Cases i
International
Management

A Focus on Emerging Markets

Stephen M. Hills

G. Keong Leong

P. Roberto Garcia

Ohio State University

West Publishing Company
Minneapolis/St. Paul   New York
Los Angeles   San Francisco

WEST'S COMMITMENT TO THE ENVIRONMENT

In 1906, West Publishing Company began recycling materials left over from the production of books. This began a tradition of efficient and responsible use of resources. Today, 100% of our legal bound volumes are printed on acid-free, recycled paper consisting of 50% new paper pulp and 50% paper that has undergone a de-inking process. We also use vegetable-based inks to print all of our books. West recycles nearly 27,700,000 pounds of scrap paper annually—the equivalent of 229,300 trees. Since the 1960s, West has devised ways to capture and recycle waste inks, solvents, oils, and vapors created in the printing process. We also recycle plastics of all kinds, wood, glass, corrugated cardboard, and batteries, and have eliminated the use of polystyrene book packaging. We at West are proud of the longevity and the scope of our commitment to the environment.

West pocket parts and advance sheets are printed on recyclable paper and can be collected and recycled with newspapers. Staples do not have to be removed. Bound volumes can be recycled after removing the cover.

Production, Prepress, Printing and Binding by West Publishing Company.

 TEXT IS PRINTED ON 10% POST CONSUMER RECYCLED PAPER    Printed with **Printwise** Environmentally Advanced Water Washable Ink

COPYRIGHT © 1996 by WEST PUBLISHING CO.
610 Opperman Drive
P.O. Box 64526
St. Paul, MN 55164–0526

ISBN 0–314–09868–2

Contents

PREFACE

Worldwide, international trade has grown manyfold in the last three decades. Most of the growth in trade has been between countries that are already industrialized, but increasingly business firms have found that their best opportunities exist in the fast industrializing economies of the world. The U.S. Department of Commerce refers to these fast growing economies as "emerging markets" and maintains a list of the top ten (currently China, Indonesia, India, South Korea, Turkey, South Africa, Poland, Argentina, Brazil, and Mexico).

American business students need current information on emerging markets, particularly since change is occurring so rapidly in each of them. Business school curriculum has not always reflected the unique challenges facing business firms in emerging markets, however. In fast growing markets, businesses may cooperate more with one another since economic growth means that competition does not have to be so sharp for market share. In older, more stable markets, what one firm gains must often be at the expense of a well known competitor.

The emerging markets of the world have other characteristics that students need to appreciate. Decision making is difficult due to the more volatile economic environment. Sudden, sharp exchange rate changes may occur without warning. Government policies regarding basic investment rules change. In some cases, policy may dictate a wholesale change from a planned to a market economy. In all these situations, strategic planning is complicated and organizations may have to redesign themselves repeatedly to match the new environments.

Rapid advances in communication, sharp declines in the costs of transportation and the increased mobility of capital have had interesting, unanticipated consequences. International competition has increased dramatically, decisions must often be made on the spot, and firms find it hard to maintain comparative advantage for very long -- with one important exception. The way in which human resources are organized and managed can help create organizational successes that are hard to imitate.

The set of cases collected here are representative of a variety of problems that managers are likely to encounter in emerging markets. The impetus for collecting the cases has come from the establishment of a Center for International Business Education and Research (CIBER) in the Fisher College of Business at the Ohio State University. The editors of the volume are all associated with the CIBER, whose focus is also on emerging markets.

Several of the cases on Mexico were prepared by MBA students in the Fisher College as part of a course that they designed for themselves in the academic year 1994-95. Students identified companies that were strongly affected by the sharp and unexpected devaluation of the Peso in 1994 and traveled to Mexico to interview top level managers in these companies. The companies have also been adjusting to new trading rules adopted through the establishment of the North American Free Trade Agreement. The adjustments these companies are making allow students to examine the interplay of government policy with business strategy.

A second set of cases focuses on problems that are inherent in countries where the economic activity of a centrally planned system is suddenly transformed to free market activity. The experiences of managers in China, Ethiopia, Hungary, and Russia are examined. Problems differ significantly from those encountered in countries with long histories of free market business practice. A final pair of cases examines interesting changes in business practices in Thailand and India.

This case book can be used in conjunction with an introductory text in International Business, or it can be used alone by instructors who want to teach the principles of international business in the context of fast emerging markets. In either case, the breadth of cases, in terms of country, culture, industry, size of firm, and business environment should provide the student with a realistic preview of what might be in store as businesses become more and more global.

We give special thanks to the CIBER staff at Ohio State, to Joe Cheng, Academic Director of International Programs, to Cheryl Ryan, CIBER Director, and to Melynda Hicks, CIBER Program Coordinator, Fanza Andriamialisoa and all those who have allowed us to include their work in this text.

Stephen M. Hills
G. Keong Leong
P. Roberto Garcia

Case 1.1 ·

FOREIGN INVESTMENT ACTIVITY AND THE MEXICAN PESO DEVALUATION OF 1994[1]

Summary

The financial environment of Mexico prior to the December, 1994 devaluation is described. Reasons for the large outflow of capital in early 1994 are examined retrospectively. The recovery plan and its anticipated consequences are analyzed. The case establishes the financial background to other cases from Mexico but also describes conditions that are all too familiar in emerging markets. Betting on emerging markets can be risky business.

Investors were once again reminded that betting on emerging markets is risky business.

On Tuesday, December 20, 1994, Mexico reversed a long-standing currency policy and allowed the peso to fall 12.7% relative to the U.S. dollar. This decision came four days after Finance Minister Dr. Jaime Serra Puche, had assured investors there would not be any change in the peso policy. Within a month, the peso lost 40% of its value. The new administration, led by President Ernesto Zedillo, blamed the devaluation and other economic problems on the resurgence of revolt in Chiapas led Indian rebels.

The economic crisis was actually a consequence of accumulated economic and political problems that coincided and led to the crisis (see Exhibit 1: Timeline of the Significant Events of 1994). Political instability, assassinations and kidnappings, uncertainty about the results of the August elections and the anticipated fear of a possible economic rupture in case of a PRI (Institutional Revolutionary Party) defeat caused significant capital outflow in Spring of 1994. The consequences of the political and social problems were, and include:

- Halt in economic growth,
- Sudden sharp increase in interest rates,
- Limiting of the availability of credit lines,
- Decrease in international reserves,
- Sharp devaluation of the peso, and
- Loss of confidence in Mexico's current administration

By March 1995, a recession was looming over Mexico's economy. The peso's fall had led to even greater economic woes: high interest rates and inflationary forces drove commercial and consumer loan default rates up. Sales of consumer goods were off 30 to 50%, as workers' salary increases were capped at 7% while

---

[1] The framework for this case was provided by Mr. Johannes Hauser, Sub Director of the German/Mexican Chamber of Commerce, in a presentation to German and Swiss financiers, and Ohio State University MBA students on March 23, 1995, in Mexico City, Mexico.

This case was written by Cheol-In Kim and Donald Murray, MBA students in 1995 in the Max M. Fisher College of Business, The Ohio State University, under the supervision of Professors Roberto Garcia, Stephen Hills, and G. Keong Leong. This case was written for class discussion and does not necessarily imply good or poor management practices.

inflation exceeded 40%. Around the world, business leaders and investors were split on their assessment of the situation. Pessimists saw a financial meltdown, but optimists anticipated a more temporary crisis.

The most devastating effects of the devaluation were the loss of confidence in the Zedillo government and the loss of belief in Mexico as a prosperous, developing country. To help the country's economy survive, Mexico requested the largest concerted, international emergency aid (US$53 billion) bailout in history.

1994's Forecast was Positive

Mexico had gone through economic crises before (see Exhibit 2: Peso History) and recovered. Since the late 1980s, Mexico's economy had shown constant improvement. Formerly state-owned businesses had been privatized and in 1994, the budget was nearly balanced. NAFTA, which went into effect January 1, 1994, opened Mexico's economy to greater foreign direct investment and global competition. NAFTA meant opportunities for increasing trade volume, higher confidence in Mexico's economic stability, increased foreign investments, decreased unemployment and an increased demand for infrastructure development.

According to the U.S. Department of Commerce, U.S. exports to Mexico were up 16.7% in the first six months of 1994, compared to the same time period one year earlier. In 1994, Mexicans bought some US$50 billion worth of American products, an amount sufficient to give the U.S. one of its largest bi-lateral trade surpluses. At that time, economists were predicting a rosy picture for Mexico's growth potential. Foreign direct investment was increasing, Mexican industries were working to become more competitive, infrastructure spending was continuing upward and 1995's growth in GDP was predicted to be 4%, compared to 0.4% in 1993, and an estimated 2.5% for 1994.

Nonetheless, Mexican investors had seen their stock investments decline 32% in 1994 when growth was expected to be nearly 40%. When the devaluation occurred, speculative investors immediately lost 12.7% of their US$75 billion holdings, and, those who kept their investments in place lost nearly 50% by March. Speculative investors were the crisis' biggest losers.

Long-term foreign direct investors suffered from lowered sales caused by the lull in the economy. However, most of these investors had wisely hedged against unforeseen changes in the exchange rate, and did not suffer the immediate reduction of holdings that short-term speculators did.

What Happened

Mexico's current account deficit was often cited as the primary cause of the peso's 1994 decline. In 1994 the current account deficit had surpassed US$28 billion, or 8% of its GDP (the U.S. current account deficit was approximately 3% of its GDP). What made Mexico particularly vulnerable before devaluation was its reliance on short-term debt instruments, called *tesobonos*,[2] to finance the deficit. Mexico had received a tremendous inflow of speculative, short term capital. In 1994, nearly three-fourths of all Mexican foreign capital was invested in highly speculative stock; only one-fourth was in direct capital investments.

On December 20, when Finance Minister Jaime Serra Puche lowered the currency's floor[3] by 53 centavos, widening the exchange rate band by 15%, the stock market began its fall. Dr. Serra commented that this step did not signify a move towards devaluation rather the move was intended as a measure to defend Mexico's

---

[2] Tesobonos are peso denominated bonds fixed to the U.S. dollar
[3] Mexico used a managing float method to control the peso's value

international reserves, which were at dangerously low levels (see Exhibit 3: International Reserve History). Market investors agreed that international reserves were low but were not convinced that this was the only reason for widening the exchange rate band. Nor did they think that the lowered exchange rate was a one-time event.

By the end of December 20, US$3.5 billion had left the country. That night the Central Bank of Mexico announced its intention to allow the peso to float freely on the market. The next morning the market opened with an exchange rate of US$1 : N$5.60. The day before, the exchange rate had been US$1 : N$3.47.

As capital flight continued, Mexico's low international reserves proved too little to shore up the peso. When federal reserves hit $5 billion during the first week of January, the government announced it would (could) no longer support the peso's value - at any level. This resulted in a peso nose-dive that led to increased capital flight and a continued decline in the value of the peso.

By the second week of January, 1995, the peso had been devalued by more than 35% and stock market shares had lost more that 20% of their value. Speculators were pulling out, exacerbating capital flight. Most direct investors stood fast, prepared to ride out the storm, but they controlled too little of the country's capital to stop the outward flow of capital.

Other factors contributed to the devaluation of the peso. Exhibits 4, 5 and 6 graphically display how key events in 1994 (refer to Exhibit 1) affected the exchange rate, interest rates and stock market performance.

The Recovery Plan

On January 3, the Zedillo administration announced an emergency package to put Mexico's economy back on track. The plan met with surprisingly little enthusiasm from the investment community. The plan called for government spending cuts of $3.7 billion (1.3% of GDP), a 7% ceiling on wage increase (an agreement reached with the labor unions), expanded privatization, no exchange controls and a suppression of price increases in the public and private sectors. In an attempt to further soothe the market, a few days later the government also promised to freeze hiring, ban state spending on real estate and new cars, and reduce budgets for official travel, phone use and other expenses.

On March 9, the government announced a new economic program:

- A value added tax (VAT) increase from 10 to 15%,
- Gasoline and electricity prices to rise immediately by 20%,
- Public sector to cut expenses by almost 10%,
- A minimum salary increase of 10% by April 1,
- Banks to be backed with a US$3 billion credit by international institutions,
- A planned restructuring of credits.

This program, some say imposed by international organizations and the U.S. government, was aimed at stabilizing the financial markets. The plan received mixed reactions from Mexico's private sector. But the only alternative to the program was to declare a suspension of payments, a move that would have meant a financial relapse similar to that experienced in the early '80s and restricted access to international financial markets.

Many analysts were concerned with the social implications of Zedillo's proposal. The Mexican population had suffered from what seemed to be a permanent reduction of purchasing power in order to battle inflation.

Mexico rested on top of a barrel of gunpowder in wait of a spark. Already, Mexicans, including the usually docile middle class, had taken to the streets in often volatile protest.

The government's preoccupation in 1995 was that uncontrolled inflation could neutralize the positive effects of the devaluation for the local export industry. The inflation rate for January and February of 1995 was 8.16%, an annual rate of 49%, and this did not take into account the inflationary effects of increases in VAT, electricity, gasoline and public service announced in March.

Effect on Foreign Companies

Foreign companies (Mexico's top three foreign investors in 1995 were the U.S., Great Britain and Germany) had extended their presence in Mexico even before NAFTA, anticipating a closer cooperation with North America and possible ties to the rest of Latin America.

How badly a company was affected by the crisis varied according to its sources of capital, whether it was a net importer or exporter, and how well it used hedging to minimize currency fluctuation risk.

A company can hedge against transaction risk by raising capital in the market in which it operates. However, many large company subsidiaries rely on parent organizations for capital inflows. This means that the company must set up balancing flows of imports and exports or use financial hedging tools to protect against unexpected currency parity shifts.

Although the International Monetary Fund (IMF) had warned Mexico that its currency was trading at an inflated rate, the IMF did not publicize this warning to the general market. Using a U.S.-Mexico, intra-country, differential inflation and interest rate calculation, (see Exhibits 7 and 8) many companies knew the peso was overvalued, and consequently hedged accordingly. Those that did not suffered significant losses.

Outlook

The most positive aspect of the devaluation was the elimination of the artificial exchange rate. The peso was now to be evaluated by the market and not manipulated by political strategies. The low peso gave the export sector increased trading capabilities. During the first two months of 1995 trade figures showed a surprisingly good performance: the deficit was US$78 million, whereas in the same period in 1994 the deficit had been US$3 billion.

In February, Mexico realized a surplus of US$452 million. However, it should be pointed out that a significant portion of this surplus was due to a drastic decrease in imports.

In 1995, many Mexican companies were unable to pay their bills or finance new supplies and equipment. This left collectors in a position of writing off uncollectable loan losses or restructuring them to a level customers could pay. Financially, in the short run no one could win. The primary consideration was to maintain long-term relations that would last, and to prosper as the crisis diminished.

In mid-February 1995, the U.S. assembled an aid package of US$49 billion for Mexico. This proposal had U.S. bipartisan support, but still met with criticism by anti-NAFTA proponents and by law makers wary of foreign entanglements. The aid did not come free of strings. Mexico had to agree to cut government spending, slow the growth of private credit, limit its money supply, and sell off more state-owned industries.

Most experts agreed that Mexico would rebound. Many business leaders predicted that full recovery would occur within two to three years. These same leaders were beginning to prepare their companies to take advantage of the expected new opportunities.

Questions for students

1.   In retrospect, should investors have been aware much sooner of the possibility for devaluation of the Peso? Why or why not?

2.   What lessons have been learned -- for the Mexican government, for short term investors, for long term investors, and for the international economic community?

3.   Effects of the devaluation have been extreme for ordinary citizens of Mexico. What are the political ramifications?

Exhibit 1: Significant Events of 1994 Leading Up to the Devaluation

Jan	Beginning of revolt in Chiapas
Feb	Kidnapping of Mr. Harp (Chairman of Banamex)
Mar 23	Assassination of Luis Donaldo Colosio (Presidential Candidate)
July	Kidnapping of Mr. Losada (Vice-President Gigante)
Aug	Excess expansion of the peso money supply during the presidential election, presumably to support the re-election of the incumbent PRI party.
Aug 21	Peaceful elections - Ernesto Zedillo Ponce de Léon (PRI) new president
Sep 28	Assassination of José Francisoco Ruiz Massieu, Secretary General of PRI (Ruiz Massieu was slated to a major player in reforming Mexico's next government)
Dec 1	Peaceful installation of the new government
Dec	Renewed political instability in the southern state of Chiapas
Dec 20	Finance Minister, Dr. Jaime Serra Puche, widens the peso's trading band

Exhibit 2: Peso History

1955 - 1976	Exchange rate fixed at 12.5 pesos to US$1 government artificially maintained rate by intervention and import controls
1976	Currency devalued to 20.5 : 1. Exchange rate holds until 1982
1982	Devalued to 38.5 : 1, then 47.5 : 1 Dual rates established, official and free-market, both quickly rose to 105 : 1
1984	Rate at 143.9 : 1
1989	Rate has climbed to 2,281 : 1
1993	Government changed decimal point, exchange rate now 3.1154 : 1
until Dec 1994	Exchange rate held above 3.4712 pesos to the dollar
Dec 20, 1994	Peso given permission to go as low as 4.0016 pesos per dollar Peso immediately drops to 4.0016 : 1
Dec 21	Free floatation of peso

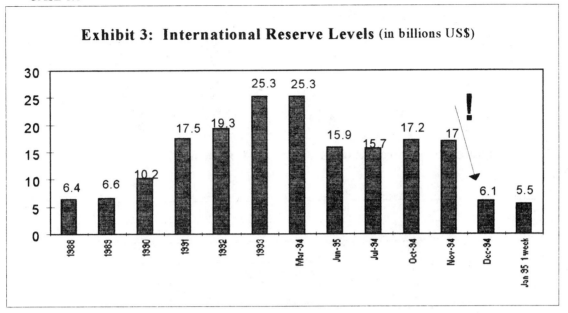

Exhibit 3: International Reserve Levels (in billions US$)

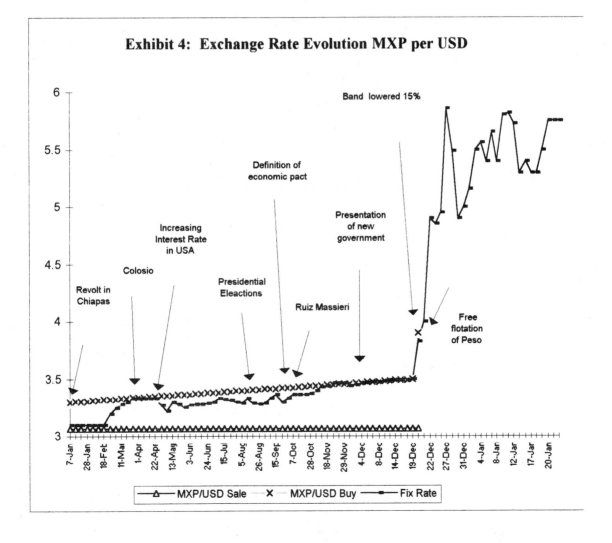

Exhibit 4: Exchange Rate Evolution MXP per USD

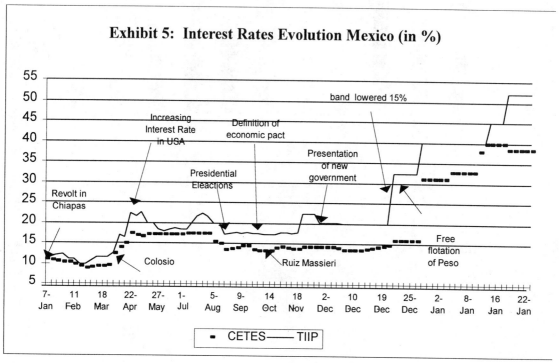

Exhibit 5: Interest Rates Evolution Mexico (in %)

Exhibit 6: Stock Market Performance

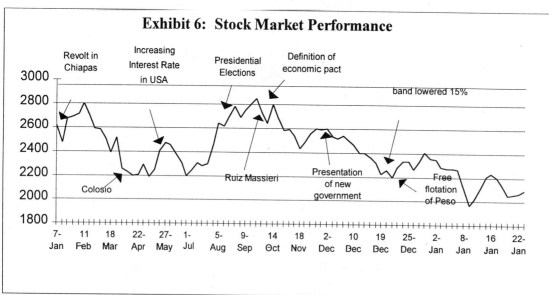

Exhibit 7: BASF Mexico's Exchange Rate Forecast

MARGEN DE SOBRE/(SUB)VALUACION DEL N$ VS. USD							
(%)					1995 Estimate		
	1980 - 92	1993	1994	Q1	Q2	Q3	Q4
Inflation Mexico	758.0%	8.0%	7.1%	42.0%	54.0%	50.0%	60.0%
Inflation USA	68.1%	2.8%	2.7%	3.0%	30.0%	3.0%	3.0%
Difference	689.9%	5.2%	4.4%	39.0%	42.0%	47.0%	57.0%
Devaluation	715.1%	4.6%	50.0%	22.1%	25.1%	30.1%	40.1%
Margin	25.2%	0.6%	-45.7%	16.9%	16.9%	16.9%	16.9%
Margin accumulation	25.2%	25.8%	-19.8%	-3.0%	-3.0%	-3.0%	-3.0%
% Change			50.0%	2.2%	25.1%	30.1%	40.1%
Exchange Rate		3.33	5	6.1	6.25	6.5	7

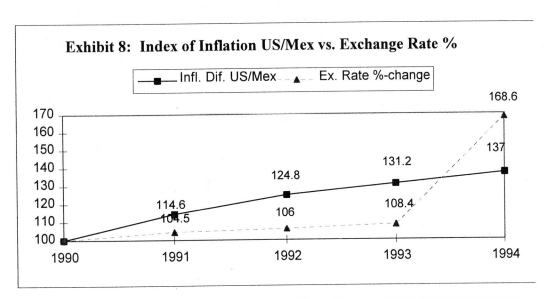

Exhibit 8: Index of Inflation US/Mex vs. Exchange Rate %

Infl. Dif. US/Mex   Ex. Rate %-change

	1991	1992	1993	1994
Peso Over-Under Valuation	9.6	17.7	21	-23.1
Inflation Mexico accumulated	18.8	11.9	8	7.1

Case 1.2

Grupo UNIKO

Summary

A Mexican auto parts firm responds to the new competitive pressures caused by an opening up of the Mexican market that has culminated in the NAFTA agreement. The case shows how UNIKO fostered an environment that was conducive to change and that maintained a focus on multiple stakeholders -its clients, shareholders, personnel and community. The management at UNIKO has taken a long term view toward what it considers a temporary comparative advantage in low wages. In preparation for increased future wages, UNIKO is investing heavily in training, is rooting itself in its community, and is using the specific knowledge of its workforce to adapt its technologies to the high quality demands of global markets.

In March of 1995, Rubén Galván, director of Grupo UNIKO (UNIKO), faced a threatening competitive and economic environment. The Mexican auto parts industry faced increasing competition due to a shrinking economy and the passage of the North American Free Trade Agreement (NAFTA). The massive devaluation of the Mexican peso spurred a financial crisis that negatively impacted most of Mexican industry. Most importantly, the economic crisis resulted in the contraction of the market for vehicles and consequently in the demand for auto parts. UNIKO had to implement a strategy that would assure the group's survival and continued performance in Mexican and international markets. Galván had to decide how to position UNIKO for global competitiveness.

Grupo UNIKO has chosen to focus on achieving long-term fundamental competitiveness through a focused corporate vision: "becoming a group of companies deploying a service spirit in an environment of continuous development and creativity." (Exhibit 1). Galván broadly defines fundamental competitiveness as the ability to satisfy and exceed customer expectations while maintaining high levels of quality and technological competence. UNIKO's customer focus, however, encompasses more than simply catering to its clients. In fact, UNIKO defines its customers as its clients, shareholders, personnel, and community (Exhibit 2). UNIKO's management believes that the group as a whole will attain fundamental competitiveness by meeting the needs of all of its customers. Therefore, UNIKO's goal is to optimize critical processes across functional areas, identified according to all of its customers' demands and needs, while maintaining high quality products and levels of technology. UNIKO must foster an environment that is conducive to change and to the implementation of its "customer focus."

Company Background

Grupo UNIKO is a collection of companies engaged in the manufacture of auto-parts for both Mexican and international original equipment manufacturers (OEMs) and distributors (aftermarket). As of 1994, exports accounted for only 20% of sales while the OEMs and aftermarket accounted for 50% and 30%, respectively. UNIKO's principal products include Constant Velocity (CV) crankshafts, pistons and related parts, pick-up boxes, valves, and valve lifters. UNIKO is composed of a number of manufacturing subsidiaries (Pistones Moresa, Vel-con, Fomasa, Morestana, Alfisa, Copresa, and Morinsa) and Tecnysia,

This case was written by Claudia Bowles, Alan Campbell, and David Englehardt, MBA students in 1995 in the Max M. Fisher College of Business, The Ohio State University, under the supervision of Professors Roberto Garcia, Stephen Hills, and G. Keong Leong. This case was written for class discussion and

Morinsa) and Tecnysia, a systems automation firm. These companies are owned by UNIK, a holding group and subsidiary of DESC, one of the largest Mexican business conglomerates (Exhibit 3).

Grupo UNIKO resulted from the restructuring of SPICER S.A. in January 1994. Before the 1994 restructuring, SPICER was a collection of auto parts companies similar to Grupo UNIKO but with a much larger product base. SPICER was a partnership between DESC and the U.S.-based DANA Corporation. The partnership's history traces back to the 1960's, when DANA Corporation joined the Senderos Trouyet Group (now DESC) in a joint venture. In January 1994, Dana Corporation decided to dilute and re-focus its investment to concentrate on its primary fields of interest. This resulted in the formation of UNIK, Grupo UNIKO's parent company, and SPICER S.A. SPICER S.A. manufactures universal joints, axles, drive-shafts, transmissions, and clutches. DANA retained 49% ownership of SPICER, and gave up its interest in all but one (Vel-con) of the companies under UNIK.

A critical feature of Grupo UNIKO is its strategic alliance and partnership with several foreign firms. UNIKO is supported by technical agreements with world leaders in the automotive industry. Its foreign technology partners include:

- TRW, U.S.A.: Shareholder of MORESA and provider of technical assistance for Valves,
- GKN, Europe: Shareholder of Vel-con and provider of technical assistance for CV joints,
- UNISIA-JECS, Japan: Provider of technical assistance for Pistons,
- FANUC, THK, and PHD, U.S.A.: Provider of technical assistance on Automation, and
- AERCOLOGY, U.S.A.: Provider of technical assistance on Environmental Control Systems.

Aside from this technical support, each of Grupo UNIKO's companies has fully developed its own technological capacity in order to provide the best combination of local resources to achieve competitive potential.

UNIKO's Total Quality Philosophy

UNIKO's total quality philosophy (Exhibit 4), shared with the parent company UNIK, dictates that the group must be committed to exceeding the expectations of its four customers (clients, shareholders, personnel, and community), and must emphasize the projection of a consistent company "image" and strategy. Total quality is related to UNIKO's vision (Exhibit 1). In addition, UNIKO's vision involves using customer perception as a platform for the improvement of plans and products and implementing processes in a reliable, structured, and systematized manner. Galván believes that enforcing UNIKO's total quality philosophy will guarantee customer satisfaction and future competitiveness.

The total quality philosophy is ingrained in the company's strategic objectives which include:

- Participation,
- Productivity,
- Zero downtime or unscheduled stops,
- Zero unrecycled scrap and rework,
- Zero iventory, and
- Zero changeover time.

Specifically, the total quality philosophy dictates the following strategies for meeting the needs of each of its customers:

Clients

Total quality demands that UNIKO provide clients with competent service, competitive price, quality, and technological creativity in manufacturing processes, product design and development.

Shareholders

UNIKO aims to meet shareholders' demands for profitability, sales growth, and image. UNIKO's management hopes to achieve a return on investment greater than 15% through long-term planning and careful preparation of investment strategies. Similarly, UNIKO hopes to increase sales by creating and implementing an integrated marketing strategy. The projection of a consistent corporate image is a critical aspect of UNIKO's competitive strategy. Ruben Galván has emphasized the importance of maintaining an image of high quality and technological competence. He has admitted that some investments in technology were made mainly to meet customers' wants and expectations, not to satisfy any overriding technical requirement. However, UNIKO also views its investments in technology and automation as a way to achieve discipline and consistency in its processes and quality.

Personnel

Because personnel are also customers, UNIKO has both a short-term and long-term vision on people development. Special emphasis is placed on building a satisfied, productive, and skilled workforce because UNIKO considers it to be the source of current and future competitive advantage. Consequently, UNIKO strives to meet the current and future needs of its workforce, emphasizing long-term people development. Long-term people development involves the use of continuous in-house training. Moreover, UNIKO makes an effort to improve the working environment in its plants, as well as to provide competitive income commensurate with skill levels. Management prefers to increase skills and consequently wages in order to improve the quality of its workforce and reduce turnover. Similarly, UNIKO provides subsidized services such as cafeterias, medical care, and safety.

Community

Ruben Galván states that UNIKO seeks to "establish roots" in the communities in which it operates. Community activities are aimed at creating a "family" environment with the families of its workers as well as other people in the community. Their "community focus" emphasizes active participation, family programs, respect for the environment, and good citizenship. Active participation entails attention to visitors, support to charities, and promotion of symposiums. Family programs include ceremonies, weekend workshops where employees' families obtain handicraft-making skills, as well as the distribution of a company newsletter, "COMMUNIKO." UNIKO places strong emphasis on preserving and protecting the environment. Its main concerns involve noise emissions, waste in the plants, and hazardous waste. The firm follows all Mexican, and most U.S., environmental standards and regulations.

Leadership

Effective leadership is a "key issue, a pivot" on which the success of these policies depends, argues Galván. Uniko stresses leadership in its managers. A "genuine leader" (Exhibit 5) is defined as honest, forward looking (able to conceptualize the vision as shown in Exhibit 1), inspiring (able to explain and energize others with that vision), and competent, both as an individual, and within teams. Uniko's corporate culture stresses an atmosphere of trust and teamwork, and managers are urged to advance it through respect for employees and with a hands-on, egalitarian supervisory style.

The Mexican Auto Parts Industry

The performance of the Mexican auto parts industry has long been tied to that of the Mexican auto industry as a whole. From 1962 to 1983, the industry was heavily restricted to promote domestic production (import-substitution strategy). For example, required local content level for domestic market vehicles was 60%. These local content restrictions, coupled with domestic ownership restrictions (majority Mexican capital), created an industry that was quite small and (by world standards), parochial and inefficient.

The industry is currently in a transitional phase characterized by a trend towards deregulation and liberalization. Beginning in 1989, automotive imports were finally allowed and many domestic content and ownership restrictions were lifted. Local content requirements in terms of value-added in Mexico were reduced to 36%. Auto imports were allowed to rise to 15% of the market in 1991, with an increase to 20% in 1993. With the passage of NAFTA, the 49% foreign ownership restriction will be lifted by 1999 and all tariffs on imports will be gradually eliminated by 2005.

NAFTA and the Mexican Peso Devaluation

NAFTA and the December 1994 Mexican peso devaluation caused UNIKO to speed up the integration and implementation of its competitive strategy. NAFTA will put added pressure on auto parts suppliers who lack adequate investment in plant, equipment, and technology and who are unable to serve all the needs of assemblers in Mexico. First, NAFTA will further liberalize the auto parts industry by reducing local content requirements, making Mexican firms vulnerable to increasing imports from foreign suppliers possessing competitively priced, higher quality products. Second, national suppliers may experience higher competition from new entrants to the industry as ownership restrictions are removed.

UNIKO's strategy to meet the challenges of NAFTA is to implement its total quality philosophy with a long-term focus. With respect to NAFTA, total quality involves maintaining UNIKO's competitive advantage and redirecting UNIKO's efforts towards export-oriented production. According to Galván, the Mexican auto part suppliers' critical short-term competitive advantage (relative to foreign competition) is low labor costs. NAFTA will open the doors for foreign investors seeking to take advantage of low Mexican labor costs. However, Galván and UNIKO's management believe that entering Mexico solely on the basis of lower labor costs is a myopic strategy. In the short run, these companies will have to cope with inadequate infrastructure, volatile political and economic conditions, and inadequate service from suppliers not up to par with world standards. Because UNIKO expects labor costs to increase in the future, it will attempt to maintain its competitive advantage by developing and modifying the talent of its people. UNIKO stresses in-house development of personnel through educational training programs.

The second tier of UNIKO's strategy is to increase export sales. The peso devaluation and its impact on the Mexican economy has underscored the importance of export sales as a hedge against currency fluctuations. In 1994, Galván recognized that UNIKO's exposure to peso fluctuations, due to its U.S. dollar denominated debt, would be offset by UNIKO's export sales. However, UNIKO cannot rely on short-term beneficial exchange rates to support sales, as this would create an unhealthy dependence on volatile currency markets.

UNIKO's export strategy targets aftermarket parts supply in the U.S., Latin America, and Europe. UNIKO is seeking to establish a niche in the aftermarket because of the transportation difficulties associated with meeting OEM needs. Most importantly, serving the aftermarket requires lower lead times and greater production flexibility. In the future, UNIKO must become fundamentally competitive, providing world class products at competitive prices.

UNIKO's Manufacturing Facilities and Corporate Philosophy

UNIKO's plants follow the focused factory design concept. Each plant is relatively small and produces an individual product line. The average workforce is around 400, and no plant has more than 1,000 employees. The relatively small size of these plants is designed to promote close, cooperative working environments and to take advantage of efficiencies of scale. A smaller workforce is more easily monitored by management. Because the company's workers are located in different facilities, instead of housed in one large plant, the strength of the worker's union is minimized. The focused factory concept is carried even further in the manufacture of pistons. Aftermarket production is located at the Morinsa factory, which is separate from OEM production at Pistones Moresa.

Ruben Galván admits that not all of UNIKO's plants have equal quality standards or similar levels of modern technology investment, that is, the same level of competitiveness. He estimates that 80% of UNIKO's plants are not up to world standards for competitiveness and that 60% are not as modern as Pistones Moresa and Vel-con (UNIKO's two most modern plants). Galván recognizes that in order for UNIKO's plants to become fundamentally competitive, they must be willing to restructure in a way that permits the implementation of the UNIKO vision. Galván believes that it is not the lag in technology that puts the less competitive plants in danger, but the inability or unwillingness of the people in the plants to accept change and adopt the total quality philosophy.

Technology and People: Finding the Appropriate Mix

Grupo UNIKO has implemented in its organization a mix of technological and human assets that it feels are appropriate for Mexico.

Technology

In the field of high-precision parts manufacturing, technology means automated machining and Computerized Numerical Control (CNC) equipment. UNIKO has an in-house division, Tecnysia, that custom develops such systems for the firm. Tecnysia upgrades and adapts second-hand U.S. and European robotics with custom electronic control systems. This approach is more cost effective than buying new systems and paying outside vendors to adapt them to UNIKO's purposes. It also allows for the development of special-use tools and machinery proprietary to the firm, an advantage not easily duplicated by its competition.

The use of an inside vendor to design systems is as much a part of UNIKO's technology development strategy as any other cost factor. UNIKO is trying to build a capability for technology. "We're trying to grow roots, not just be a low-cost opportunity," says Ruben Galván.

UNIKO needs to use automated manufacturing systems. Automated systems create quality and, when properly designed and configured, can perform complex machining operations at high speed without error. However, the "atmosphere of discipline" that automation creates for the customer is equally important. Many customers demand a high level of automation, because automation is perceived as a hallmark of quality. Customer perceptions and needs must drive improvements. This is part of UNIKO's quality policy. The use of in-house technology also develops workforce skills.

People

UNIKO believes in investing in its workforce. Training is a primary component of this policy. At the firm's Cedei training centers, workers receive basic theory training in pneumatics, hydraulics, electronics, and electrical and mechanical systems. This training starts before they ever step on to the factory floor. They also receive instruction on how to operate machinery and controls. Most employees also receive extensive diagnostic and preventative maintenance training. Such training in both theory and systems avoids the information obsolescence which is common in machine-specific instruction programs.

Tecnysia works with line employees to design and install new equipment and systems. This process requires knowledgeable employees with broad-based skills. Workers are encouraged to redesign their own jobs, in order to increase both efficiency and quality. This demands high skill levels. Furthermore, implementing the firm's quality philosophy requires that key processes be continuously updated. Continuous upgrading of manufacturing, design, and development processes are required to satisfy the needs of UNIKO's clients.

Outside observers still might wonder why UNIKO has invested so much in its workers, given the low Mexican wage rates and huge labor pool. Labor costs are a big advantage for UNIKO (vis-a-vis) U.S. and European competitors). But the firm's leadership has realized that this advantage is not a long-term one. As the Mexican economy develops, Mexican labor rates will eventually rise to parity with those in the industrialized world. In line with the firm's ambition to become a long-term leader, it must develop labor as a resource and not as a commodity. "Training is the key to our development," says Galván.

In order to retain skilled workers, UNIKO realizes that compensation is an important factor. Employees are rewarded through initial hourly pay of over three times the national minimum wage, with a regular series of increases, a program of subsidized meals through the company cafeteria, free comprehensive health care, family education, and limited profit sharing.

Highly trained workers are valuable. Good benefits help keep them. UNIKO has largely succeeded in its goal to retain its human investments. Company-wide, UNIKO's employees stay an average of 8-10 years.

Plant working environment is also an important factor in employee retention and motivation. The firm does not use any type of time-based supervision. Management has discovered that the timecard system, formerly used throughout the firm, cost more to implement than the absenteeism it was designed to curtail. Current absenteeism levels are below industry standards.

UNIKO has discovered that its employees are concerned about the safety and environment of their working area. The company uses sensor technology and extensive training to avoid on-the-job accidents. Working areas are kept clean, are well lit by natural and artificial light, and are decorated with plants and artwork created by employees and their families at the company-run continuing education facilities. Managers make themselves approachable to line employees by involving themselves in day-to-day plant floor operations. Galván espouses management by "walking around." He believes that his managers must maintain regular contact with operations to detect problems as soon as they occur. A good manager must, in Galván's words, develop "a sense of smell" for trouble.

A Closer Look: Pistones Moresa and Vel-con

Pistones Moresa and Vel-con are two of UNIKO's most modern, technologically advanced plants.

Pistones Moresa

The Pistones Moresa plant is located in Celaya, about 260 Km from Mexico City. It is a modern facility which produces aluminum pistons for original equipment manufacturers (Exhibit 5). Most of the automotive companies in Mexico, including Chrysler, Nissan, GM, Ford, and Volkswagen are customers of Pistones Moresa.

The plant is maintained as a clean, open, well-lit facility. Artwork from employees is displayed in offices and on various walls throughout the factory. Clean, lively fish tanks can be seen from many of the offices. The plant atmosphere helps to maintain positive employee morale and provides an impression of quality and professionalism to both employees and visitors.

Piston Manufacturing Process

The piston manufacturing process consists of 1) production of piston castings and 2) machining of the castings.

1) Production of piston castings

Pistons are cast from aluminum alloy of specified composition. Currently, castings used are produced at the plant or are shipped from UNIKO's Alfisa plant in Huehuetoca. Management plans to eventually produce all of the required castings on site.

The castings made at the plant are produced in one of two automated cellular stations. Each station contains three large vats of liquid aluminum alloy mounted on a rotating platform. A pair of robotic arms alternately removes liquid from one of the vats while the others are refilled and tested for proper aluminum alloy composition. Testing is performed in a nearby room with state of the art chemical and optical analysis. Each robotic arm pours liquid alloy into a casting mold. Two molds, each with four cavities, are alternately filled by a single robotic arm. This alternate filling speeds up the manufacturing process since one mold can be filled while the other cools to the proper temperature. Once a mold has cooled to the proper temperature, the castings are automatically removed.

2) Machining of the castings

The majority of the plants' operations are concentrated on machining the rough castings to specified dimensions. The plant contains a total of 12 machining lines: six manual, four semi-automatic, and two recently installed fully-automatic lines (Exhibit 6). The semi-automatic lines are set up in a U shaped structure which allows individual workers to perform more than one operation. The closest worker shown in Exhibit 6 is removing pistons from the end of the line. Once this is performed, the worker will turn around and load up rough castings onto the beginning of the line. The other workers in this cell perform multiple operations in the same manner.

Two technicians are required to maintain the operation of the automatic lines. Each of the machine stations has its own control panel and lights to indicate if the machine is running properly (green) or if there is some sort of problem (red). If a problem develops in one of the machines, the entire line is shut down until it can be resolved by one of the technicians.

To maintain tight tolerances in the final product, and to avoid any expansion or contraction of the metal, the pistons must be kept at a constant temperature of 20^0 C throughout the milling process. The pistons are bathed in a solvent solution prior to each stage in the machining process, and held in the solution until they reach the exact temperature for machining. The solution is also used to cool the cutting heads.

Once the machining is completed, workers check each of the pistons to ensure they are within the required weight tolerances. If the weight is too great, small amounts of material are machined from the piston in order to reduce its weight to a specified level.

Workers at the end of the lines insert offset pins (produced at UNIKO's Copresa plant near Mexico city) into the pistons and then package them for shipping.

Additional Characteristics of the Plant

The automated machining lines are not dedicated to individual customers. In fact, minimal changeover time on these lines allows several models to be produced during a given shift. Changeover time for the manual lines is much greater, which results in more dedication of these lines to specific products. Pistones Moresa is continuing to work towards a goal of 100% flexibility in all of its lines.

To maintain levels of product quality on the manual lines comparable to that of the automated lines, the manual lines are operated at a slower production rate. The manual lines run at about half of the speed of the fully automated line. By operating at a level lower than the maximum possible rate, workers are able to maintain required levels of product quality.

Pistones practices predictive (not preventive) maintenance to keep machines up and running. Engineers chart equipment performance to head off the kind of irregular or atypical failures that preventive maintenance in unable to forestall.

Vel-con

The Vel-con plant is located near Pistones Moresa and produces Constant Velocity (CV) joints for front-wheel-drive and four-wheel-drive vehicles. Unlike pistons, CV joints are composed of a number of different components assembled at the plant. The facility produces in excess of 120 different product assemblies. Vel-con has an information center inside the main factory floor entrance where employees can peruse sales, quality, and product charts, along with other displays and reviews. The facility has a similar environment to that of Pistones, with extensive natural lighting and a large amount of greenery.

Market Information

Vel-con produces 55% of its products for the original equipment manufacturer market and 45% for the aftermarket. They have a 97% OEM market share, and control 87% of the aftermarket. Aftermarket parts are manufactured to the same exacting quality standards demanded by OEM consumers. Price is the primary selling point in the aftermarket.

In general, domestic (Mexican) steel quality is lower than that of other countries, so most steel bar stock is imported. The plant has almost 60 suppliers and over 153 distributors for its finished products. Average inventory for finished goods is 30 days.

Production Techniques

Production is not labor intensive, but instead relies heavily on automation. Emphasis is placed on having one interrelated and flexible production line rather than separate stations. Each line can handle components for up to four different types of joints at a time. Components are tracked through a system of magnetically coded assembly platforms, each of which carries four units. Vel-con is currently working on the development and installation of parallel assembly lines to increase the flexibility of this process.

Vel-con conducts most of its development work separate from Tecnysia. The in-house engineering staff allows the division to move from idea to finished process in about two months. Vel-con also charts each employee's skill level, and encourages them to learn as many skills as possible. This allows management to move workers from one task to another in response to changes in production volume or special setup needs.

Environmental Issues

All of the plant's waste products are thoroughly treated. The machine tools are constantly bathed in a solution of water and a chemical solvent which carries away heat and metal shavings. At a plant facility, the shavings are collected for recycling and the solvent is extracted for reuse. Oil, which is washed from the tools, is removed in a bacterial holding tank. The remaining wastewater is settled out and chemically purified. The facility's power plant meets EPA emissions standards.

A Competitive Balance

UNIKO has adopted a mixture of high technology and human skill in its production processes. Advanced technology is essential to survival in the newly globalized auto parts market. Skilled personnel give the firm flexibility and allow it to constantly update and improve its processes. Through a combination of strategic alliances, export-derived capital, and forward focused leadership, UNIKO is reinventing itself. It is in transition from being a fairly typical producer of highly technical products in a parochial market to becoming a world-class fabricator of competitive parts for global assemblers. UNIKO is adapting to the changing needs and faces of its customers, becoming, in the process, a customer-driven company. UNIKO's leadership realizes the promise and perils posed by NAFTA and is making the investments
necessary to weather these and other uncertainties of the Mexican economy. The ultimate challenge, however, is for all of UNIKO's plants to complete the transition and become globally competitive.

Questions for students

1. The director of Grupo UNIKO, Rubén Galván, does not believe that new technology and its financing are the main problems confronting the Mexican auto parts industry. In contrast, he believes that the most important problem is human resources. Show how the case reflects Galvan's belief.

2. Previous policies of import substitution in Mexico allowed auto parts firms to develop in an environment in which they did not have to be terribly sensitive to their customers. Firms were relatively paternalistic and the workforce was not presumed to have much interest in managerial decisions. Show how UNIKO has departed from these old assumptions in some instances but in others reflects past practices.

EXHIBIT 1

UNIKO'S VISION

- To become a group of companies deploying a customer service spirit in an environment of continuous development and creativity.

- Our customers' perception of the quality and competitiveness of the company will be forged with the honesty, congruency, and enthusiasm of the leaders.

- The processes of any kind, applied to satisfy our customers' expectations will be reliably structured and systemized to guarantee success.

EXHIBIT 2

UNIKO'S CUSTOMERS

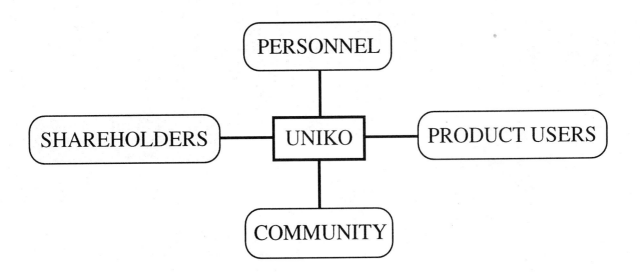

EXHIBIT 3

MEXICAN BUSINESS CONGLOMERATE DESC

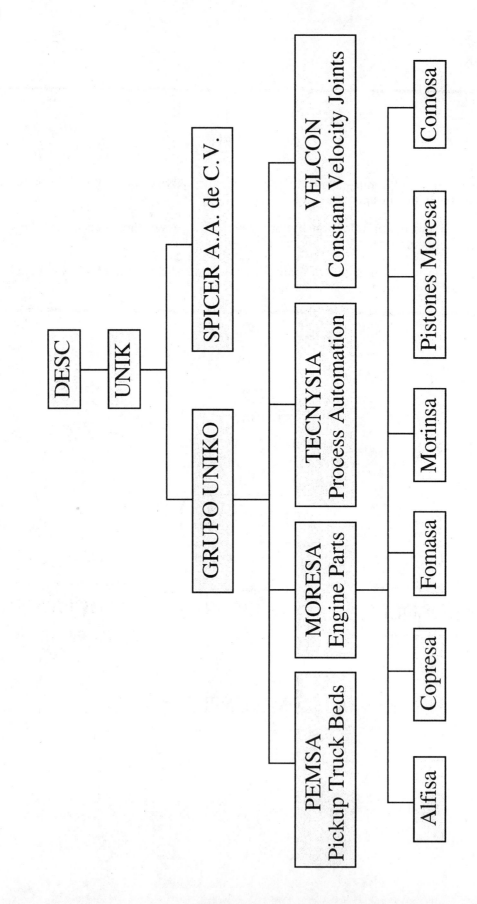

EXHIBIT 4

UNIKO'S QUALITY POLICY

- To serve our customers is the only reason for existence of the company.

- Our customers' perception must be the platform to design improved plans.

- The expectation of our customers must be exceeded.

- It is the leader's task to establish the conditions, plans, structure, and system to assure customer satisfaction.

- It is everyone's task to apply our best effort as individuals and through team work to achieve the goals.

- The key processes shall be robust and continuously updated to optimize response time and value to our customers.

EXHIBIT 5

UNIKO'S LEADERSHIP

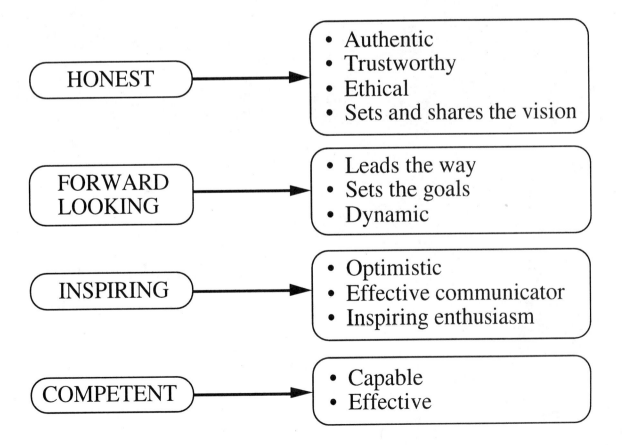

Case 1.3

AKAKI GARMENT FACTORY

Summary

After seventeen years under a socialist system, a new Ethiopian government changed policy and launched an economic restructuring program that would reintroduce a market-oriented economy. The first step was to give relative autonomy to public enterprises in managing their own business affairs. Although the management of the Akaki Garment Factory (AGF) was pleased with the change to a market economy, they found the transition tougher than initially anticipated. After nearly a year in a more autonomous setting, management found that finished goods inventories were higher, orders were lower, and product quality was still poor. Despite a reduction in shifts from three to two, the enterprise struggled to keep the workforce fully employed. The government announced it would discontinue subsidizing unprofitable firms and that unprofitable enterprises would be sold or liquidated. AGF's management is taking this warning seriously and is exploring how to ensure the survival of the enterprise in this new drastically changed business environment.

The Akaki Garment Factory (AGF) was established in 1970 by Fuji Spinning Company Ltd. of Japan, under the name of General Textile and Garment Company of Ethiopia. Its primary purpose was to produce general textile products, including knitted and ready-made garments to supply the fast growing domestic market in Ethiopia. The outputs consisted of shirts, trousers, overalls and bed sheets. During the 1960s and early 1970s, Ethiopia attracted many foreign investors due to its stable government, robust economic growth and its large population. (Ethiopia is the third most populous nation in Africa after Nigeria and Egypt.)[1]

Akaki became an instant success and, in 1973, it started making preparations to expand operations so that it could also export products to neighboring African countries. At the beginning of 1974, however, the political climate in Ethiopia changed drastically. In February 1974, a populist revolution swept the country and, in September 1974, a group of junior military officers deposed Emperor Haile Selassie (who had ruled Ethiopia for more than 50 years).

The military regime adopted a socialist ideology and introduced several radical economic policies. It nationalized all major manufacturing and service industries as well as rural and urban land. The government monopolized domestic and foreign trade, fixed prices for most products including agricultural outputs, initiated collectivization of agriculture, and launched a highly controversial forced resettlement program in which tens of thousands of peasants were forcibly removed from their villages and resettled in other regions of the country.

---

[1] The estimated population as of 1994 was about 54 million.

This case study was prepared by Tigineh Mersha, Ph.D., University of Baltimore for class discussion and does not necessarily imply either good or poor management practices. This study has been funded, in part, by the Center for International Business Education and Research (CIBER), College of Business and Management, University of Maryland, College Park MD 20742

To facilitate its centralized management of the economy, the regime established ten corporations, and all economic enterprises in the nation were placed under the control of one of these corporations. For example, all hotels were placed under the management of the Ethiopian Hotels Corporation; all companies in the textile industry were placed under the management of the National Textile Corporation; etc. The corporations acted as headquarters, with the various enterprises placed under them the subsidiaries. The corporations performed all the major managerial functions while the managers of the individual enterprises implemented policies and directives made in corporate headquarters.

In its effort to reduce unemployment, the government routinely assigned workers to the organizations even when the managers did not request additional help. For example, all college and trade school graduates were assigned to some organization. The managers would simply be informed to expect a specified number of new workers by a certain date. At times, the managers would resist receiving additional workers, arguing that they had no place for them; nevertheless, they would be "persuaded" to accept the assigned workers. This resulted in a bloated workforce in all state-owned enterprises (SOEs).

During the socialist era, a critical measure of performance was the extent to which managers met production quotas mandated by the central plan. Moreover, a severe shortage of consumer goods in the country encouraged mass production without regard to quality. The management system involved a bureaucratic process geared toward attaining the political objectives of the socialist state rather than enhancing the efficiency and effectiveness of the organization. The lack of transparency in conducting official business and the absence of enforceable control mechanisms resulted in unbridled corruption. Consequently, most SOEs operated at a loss, and required heavy subsidies by the state to keep them afloat, thus draining public resources.

In May 1991, the socialist regime was defeated by a militant opposition group called the Ethiopian People's Revolutionary Front (EPRDF). A year later, EPRDF initiated an economic restructuring program that would dismantle the socialist economic structure and transform the economy to a market system. An important first step in the economic restructuring process was to give more management autonomy to the various enterprises by breaking down the large corporations that had been created by merging several smaller firms.

The National Textile Corporation, which controlled all textile firms in Ethiopia, was dissolved and the production units within it were reorganized as "independent" public enterprises, each led by its own board of directors. Earlier, the government had decreed that each board would consist of six-to-nine members, two-thirds appointed by the government and the remaining one-third elected by the workers.

Initiating the privatization process brought about several changes in the way the enterprises were managed. During the socialist era, the government (through the corporations) arranged for the supply of the needed raw materials; informed each enterprise what to produce; how much and when; and distributed the finished goods. With the launching of privatization, all that changed. Each public enterprise was expected to develop its own products, purchase its own raw materials, set prices for its products, determine its production requirements and conduct its own marketing. Although these are basic managerial functions for any firm in a free market system, they were new to most enterprise managers during Ethiopia's transitional period. The new managerial functions seemed daunting to the newly "empowered" management teams in most enterprises. The problem was exacerbated by the fact that the managers were not adequately prepared for the change.

The most highly trained and experienced managers were working in the large corporation offices during the socialist era. With the dissolution of the corporations, most senior managers were fired and only a few were reassigned to other management positions. Some criticized the new government for not using the skills and experience of the senior managers, instead of letting them go. Supporters of the government contended that managers of the dissolved corporations were heavily involved in corrupt activities along with the leaders of the socialist government and, therefore, had to go.

With privatization, the rules of the management game changed dramatically among Ethiopian enterprises. Meeting a production quota was no longer the major performance measure. It was no longer possible to sell finished goods to another government-owned agency and expect payment at a fixed price, regardless of quality. The newly created public enterprises had to bid for new orders, and had to be competitive both in price and quality to win new business. The new government announced that it would discontinue subsidies to poorly performing enterprises. The enterprise's survival was thus contingent on its performance and, for the first time in nearly two decades, ensuring the enterprise's financial health became a serious concern for its management. This realization created additional pressure on the part of enterprise managers to improve quality and productivity, to identify new markets and distribution channels, and to streamline operations for more satisfactory financial results.

Granting management autonomy to State-owned enterprises did not mean the end of government influence in management decisions. By appointing two-thirds of the board members, and by requiring prior approval of each public enterprise's operating and capital budgets, the government exerted effective control over enterprise activities. Moreover, top managers were appointed only with the overt or covert blessing of government authorities. Most more-experienced managers were terminated and new managers were appointed. Some have complained that appointments to many key management and board positions in public enterprises were politically-motivated.

By November 1994, when this case was prepared, the economic restructuring process was still evolving, and not all policies of the socialist regime had been overhauled. For example, the "no lay off" policy which guided all state-owned enterprises during the socialist era was still in effect. So were many other aspects of the collective agreement negotiated under the socialist regime. Though privatization was being discussed, no public enterprise had been sold, as of November 1994. The government's influence in the management of each enterprise was evident, causing some to support a speed-up of the privatization process. Others, argued that economic restructuring in Ethiopia had already gone too far and had contributed to increased tensions, had created job insecurity and had increased unemployment. While there seemed to be a consensus on the need to dismantle the socialist system and to restructure the economy, debate continued over how this should be achieved.

AGF UNDER SOCIALISM

As indicated above, the previous socialist regime had organized the various manufacturing, service and agricultural enterprises into ten large corporations. The General Textile and Garment Company of Ethiopia was renamed the Akaki Garment Factory and was placed under the management of the National Textile Corporation. For AGF, socialism brought not only a new name and new ownership, but also a new major customer. In accordance with the socialist regime's centrally planned economy, the different textile enterprises in the country were required to specialize in the production of certain types of products. Because of its experience in the manufacture of shirts and trousers, AGF's primary assignment became the production of uniforms for the Ethiopian military. This brought significant changes in management strategy and in the culture of the organization. Management no longer found it necessary to keep track of changing market conditions and customer needs. Because its production strategy shifted from "production to inventory" to "production to specific customer order," AGF no longer found it necessary to monitor market changes in style in the fast changing textile industry. With the military as its sole customer, its strategic focus became the on-time delivery of a highly limited line of products. [On the basis of negotiations made between the military and the National Textile Corporation (NTC)], AGF would simply be informed how much to produce and when to produce it. Under the new structure, it was NTC that made all important managerial decisions. For example, NTC approved all capital expenditures, raw materials purchases, and it negotiated the price of AGF products. All AGF products were distributed by a government-owned distribution agency. Hiring, firing and salary increases generally required prior approval from the Corporation.

Managers found it difficult to discipline workers. In fact, sometimes enterprise managers were fired or transferred in reaction to worker protests against them. Many managers were harassed by workers, who had overt and covert approval of the government. Realizing the clout that the labor unions had with the government, many managers tried to avoid confrontation with workers by looking the other way, in spite of declining performance and poor work discipline.

As the socialist regime found itself embroiled in civil war, the size of its army increased greatly, requiring AGF to produce the necessary uniforms. The enterprise increased the number of shifts from one to two, and then to three. Still, it did not always have sufficient capacity to meet the required production of the uniforms, in which case AGF would sub-contract some of the orders to independent entrepreneurs.

Before AGF was nationalized, daily output averaged 2,000 shirt-equivalents per line using 65 assembly and 30 preparatory workers. Under the socialist regime, the number of direct production workers per line remained essentially the same (90 workers compared to 95 workers before nationalization). However, productivity declined by 75 percent to 500 shirt-equivalents per line per day. As the socialist regime encountered increased resistance, it significantly increased the size of the military force and demanded more uniforms. The pressure to meet delivery due dates led to the relaxation of the quality standards set under Japanese management.

The socialist regime's policy impacted AGF in other ways as well. Due to the regime's desire to maximize employment headcounts, new workers were often assigned to different organizations regardless of whether they were needed. Thus, a number of workers were forced upon AGF. By 1985, the number of workers, compared with 1972, increased by 158 percent. However, production increased only by 90 percent (from about 738,000 to 1,406,000 shirt-equivalents). In 1991 production was 2.2 million shirt-equivalents with a workforce size of 1578 (Table 1). In October 1994, production fell to 584,000 shirt-equivalents, but the number of workers still stood at nearly the same level (1,521 workers).

AGF purchased its major raw material (fabric) from other government-owned enterprises. Often, it would find a variation in the quality of the fabric it acquired from these suppliers. This included texture inconsistencies, visible wrinkles, missing threads, etc. Good quality fabric was hard to get from domestic suppliers. Management knew that imported fabric would be of higher quality, but foreign exchange restrictions made fabric imports impossible. All domestic suppliers were state-controlled enterprises that reported to the National Textile Corporation. The domestic suppliers often cited problems, beyond their control as the real cause of the quality-related problems, including outdated and ill-maintained machinery; poor quality of raw materials; unmotivated workforce and government bureaucracy. Interestingly, the production manager at AGF sympathized with their problems.

THE CURRENT SITUATION

In 1992, the new government initiated an economic restructuring process, and the ten corporations created by the socialist regime to facilitate centralized control of the nation's economic activity were dismantled. Accordingly, AGF became an autonomous public enterprise. A board of directors consisting of six members was established to direct AGF. Four of the board members were appointed by the government and two were elected by the workers. Government appointees to the AGF board changed three times in less than two years. At a crucial time, high turnover in board membership left AGF without effective leadership and guidance for nearly two years.

In the socialist era, AGF had one main customer--the Ministry of Defense. AGF shipped all its products to a government controlled distribution agency at a predetermined price. The management at AGF had little concern about strategic planning, market uncertainties, price fluctuations, or materials sourcing. All of these were done by the NTC. The primary challenge for AGF was to meet production due dates.

With the demise of socialism, AGF managers find themselves in a whole new ball game. NTC has been dismantled and AGF is a semi-autonomous public enterprise. It must identify its own markets, develop its own fashion designs, acquire its own raw materials, and plan its own production. AGF began to face competition even for its bread-and-butter business--the production of military uniforms. Government subsidies stopped and management faced the possibility of liquidation or sale of the firm. Major challenges confronting AGF during the transitional period included the following:

Large Finished Goods Inventory: At its peak during the socialist regime, AGF produced 2.2 million shirt-equivalents and sometimes had difficulty meeting such a high level of demand working *three shifts, seven days a week.* To meet delivery requirements, AGF sub-contracted with local entrepreneurs. As of October 1994, demand had sunk to slightly over one-fifth of the 1989 level and managers were finding it difficult to keep two shifts busy. Inventory was extraordinarily high, partly because of plans developed during the socialist regime, and partly because foreign textile products out-competed AGF's products in both price and quality.

Lack of Demand: Under the new government AGF was no longer the sole supplier of military uniforms; it had to compete for the business. Because of many years' experience in uniform production, AGF was well-positioned to compete successfully in this market. Nevertheless, in its first test of competition in seventeen years, AGF lost to a foreign competitor (in 1993). In another bid for army uniforms in 1994, it was awarded two large orders--72,000 uniforms for the police force and 100,000 for the army. But, there were no assurances that such orders would keep coming.

Excess Workforce: A major source of concern to management was the enormous cost of maintaining the excess workforce. Keeping workers on payroll with insufficient production activity had a crippling effect on AGF's performance. As can be noted from Tables 1 and 2, production volume in 1994 was about 27% of the 1991 level, without a corresponding change in the size of the workforce. This placed management in an intractable dilemma. On the one hand, it believed that mass layoff of excess workers was socially and morally unacceptable, and could have political fall-outs. On the otherhand, economic realities demanded it. Without drastic actions, the enterprise would go under.

Labor laws in Ethiopia promulgated during the socialist regime were clearly slanted toward the workers. The collective agreement stipulated that workers should have salary increases as long as the firm reported a profit. It did not, however, specify how much the increase should be. The collective agreement did not allow for worker layoffs. Laws constrained the enterprise in dealing with the workers effectively. The result was lax work discipline, low productivity, and high absenteeism. For example, it was not uncommon to close down a line due to excessive absenteeism. To prevent shutting down two or more lines, the foremen would sometimes "cannibalize" one line in order to keep others running.

Attitude Toward Quality: For nearly seventeen years, AGF produced uniforms that were used by young conscripts. Neither the soldiers nor the military leaders were too concerned about the quality of uniforms, though they were concerned about delivery schedules. In the new environment, quality became an important consideration. Dislodging old attitudes about quality among the veteran workers (most of whom had been with AGF for over a decade) posed a formidable challenge.

New Product Strategy: Entering the non-military consumer market added to the complexity. When AGF produced for the military, design changes were seldom required, and AGF had only two people in its design department. In October 1994, one of the designers was lured away by a competing shirt manufacturer. compete effectively in the fast changing garment industry, AGF would have to introduce innovative designs and continually upgrade the design of its older products. But designers were in extremely short supply domestically and management was not sure if AGF could attract the high caliber designers they needed.

One of the executives summed up the challenges facing AGF as follows:

> "Under socialism there was insatiable demand for our products. The military was engaged in a long civil war for which tens of thousands of young conscripts were needed. We were the sole supplier of uniforms to these soldiers. Now, the total size of the army and police is fewer than one-quarter of what it was at the beginning of 1991. We are not certain that we will continue to supply even this highly reduced force. We have to compete to produce the uniforms. For years, we did not have to worry about what to produce, how much and when. All that information was provided to us, and all we had to do was churn out the uniforms as fast as we could. We had no major concerns about getting the materials, how much they would cost, and what price we would charge. All that was predetermined. Now we are expected to find a market for our products, to compete for new contracts, to source the raw materials, to negotiate our own prices, to plan our capacity based on demand forecasts, etc. We are stuck with hundreds of workers hired during peak production years, and laying off these workers is the last thing we want to do. It is a real dilemma. Balancing management's responsibilities to the firm with the moral and social obligations to the workers is a real challenge. Should we now keep hundreds of excess workers on our payroll to avoid cutting them off at the risk of bankrupting the firm, or risk the agony of firing them in order that we can save AGF from going under? In view of the socio-cultural and political environment in which we operate, this is a real tough call to make."

Questions for students

1.   Who are the major players in the organization?

2.   How free are the managers to make significant changes in the organization and thereby increase its profit? What are the constraints on change?

3.   How did the granting of more management autonomy change the responsibility of the enterprise managers compared with their tasks during the socialist regime?

4.   What should be done about surplus workers.?   What are the social, political, and economic ramifications of the decision? (discuss both the possibility of a mass lay-off and a gradual shedding of only some of the workforce)

5.   Considering all the available facts, what should the management at AGF do?

Table 1

AKAKI GARMENT FACTORY
EMPLOYMENT

Budget year	No. of Employees
1972	521
1985	1347
1986	1342
1987	1354
1988	1365
1989	1272
1990	1264
1991	1578
1992	1567
1993	1556
1994	1521

Table 2

AKAKI GARMENT FACTORY
SALES AND PROFITS

Budget	Sales (in shirt equivalent)	Profits (Etheopian Birr)
1985	1,406,000	2,799,524
1986	1,437,165	3,116,108
1987	2,360,178	2,991,418
1988	2,444,475	1,794,086
1989	2,685,633	5,181,609
1990	3,331,117	5,877,918
1991	2,513,754	5,430,730
1992	626,000	585,961
1993	928,833	1,223,055
1994	579,746	211,811

Table 3

AKAKI GARMENT FACTORY
PLANNED AND ACTUAL OUTPUT

Budget Year	Planned Output	Actual Output
1985	1,330,000	1,405,560
1986	1,355,000	1,516,490
1987	1,387,000	2,044,302
1988	1,500,000	2,143,090
1989	1,500,000	2,128,762
1990	1,500,000	2,197,995
1991	1,500,000	2,728,221
1992	1,072,000	830,000
1993	881,000	863,000
1994	961,000	584,000

Case 1.4

BANGKOK GARMENT COMPANY, LTD.

Summary

This case concerns the formulation of manufacturing strategy in a garment plant producing men's knitted sports shirts that is located in Southeast Asia. This company is a division of one of the largest conglomerates in Thailand. Bangkok Garment serves both domestic and export markets in an environment characterized by intense global competition. The strategy issues involve: market and product selection, alignment between marketing and manufacturing strategy, process choice, and investments in infrastructure.

Mr. Mana, the Managing Director of Bangkok Garment, is preparing a review of the strategic plans for the sportswear business for presentation to the firm's Board of Directors. This includes a review of the firm's marketing and manufacturing strategy view in light of the recent penetration of Chinese garment manufacturers into the world-wide sportswear market. As Mr. Mana began the review, he wondered whether the firm should shift its emphasis concerning the markets currently targeted by the company. Furthermore, he realized that any changes in marketing strategy would, no doubt, necessitate new investment in manufacturing. The Board of Directors would be pressing for specific recommendations, and the justification, for any further investment in manufacturing.

Background

Bangkok Garment Company is part of one of the largest conglomerates in Thailand. The parent corporation, Rueng, produces a wide variety of products, many of which are consumer goods. Bangkok Garment represents a relatively small part of Rueng's overall sales.

The garment arm is a wholly integrated entity, taking raw material and spinning it into yarn, doing the weaving and knitting, finishing the fabric, manufacturing the garment, and marketing the garments at both wholesale and retail levels. The garment manufacturing operation began twenty-five years ago by selling in the domestic market. As garment sales continued to grow, and as the Thailand economy occasionally faltered, the company found it advisable to begin exporting their products. Today over half of the company's garment sales are in the export market. Initially, export sales consisted entirely of sub-contract manufacturing to marketers of branded goods. Over time the company acquired the rights to some of these manufacturers and markets licensed brands which are amongst the most popular in Thailand.

Sportswear

Bangkok Garment has two primary product lines, knit and woven garments. Both of these products are

---

sold through the same distribution channels so they use a common merchandising department. The factories, however, each have their own organizations and operate as cost centers. The organization chart for the company is shown in Exhibit 1. The factory manager for sportswear, Mr. Kittikachorn, oversees operations employing a total of 352 people, most of whom are concentrated in production, as shown in Exhibit 2.

This year the company's sportswear sales were in excess of $6 million. Currently, 70% of the unit sales were for export; although the forecast is for this percentage to decline to 60% over five years. This is largely due to strong growth in domestic sales and a flattening trend in export sales, as shown in Exhibit 2.

The product line produced and marketed by this company is quite wide, including knit, casual shirts in both polo and T-shirt design, long and short sleeve, natural and synthetic fibers, Jersey and Pique fabrics, and in a variety of striped and solid patterns. The factory has the capability of using silk screen and embroidery to provide additional product variety.

Domestic Sales

Market: The men's sportswear market in Thailand represents over $200 million in sales at the retail level. Approximately 70% of these sales occur at what might be called the middle level of price and quality. These products are sold at retail through department stores. All of Bangkok's products serve this part of the market.

The casual wear segment of the Thailand market has experienced strong growth in recent years, and many new brands have entered the market. The growth has been due to the younger generation of Thailand people dressing more casually, and to changing tastes among older men. Today, one can often finds businessmen in Thailand wearing knit shirts to the office. Several years ago this phenomena would not have occurred. The shift to a more casual lifestyle will have very positive effects on the knitwear market, but may cause problems for the woven side of Bangkok's business.

Outlets: Knit shirts in the middle level of the market are predominately sold through department stores. A small portion of these garments are sold through pro-shops at golf clubs, tennis clubs, fitness centers, etc. An even smaller portion are sold through sporting goods stores. A recent phenomena in Thailand is the opening of brand specific stores by companies like Nike, Benetton, and Puma. These companies have the ability to concentrate their sales in one store and to feature wide varieties of apparel, shoes, bags and other types of sports equipment.

Department stores in Thailand often operate as leasing companies. Many of them own very valuable retail space which they in turn rent to owners of branded merchandise. The value of this retail space is determined by the store's reputation, the location of the particular branch of the store, and the attractiveness of the store itself.

The company owning the brand contracts for a certain amount of floor space in a particular store location. In exchange for that space the company pays the department store approximately one-third of the retail price.[1] The company owning the brand hires and trains the employees[2] on the floor, owns and maintains all

---

[1] In the market a rough rule of thumb is that 1/3 of the retail price goes to the department store, 1/3 goes to marketer of the product, and 1/3 goes to the manufacturer.
[2] Company employees selling product in a department store are called PC's (personal consultants).

of the product inventory, and must buy, install, and maintain all of the display equipment and fixtures. The total investment in a single department of one department store location can be in the tens of thousands of dollars.

As part of their contract with the store, the tenant company agrees to maintain sales at a certain level for its allocated space. These sales are reviewed monthly and failure to maintain the requisite levels of sales may result in the loss of a preferred location within the store, or the loss of the space entirely. To add to the problems of these companies, the more aggressive department stores are now introducing their own brands. All of this adds up to a very competitive market for the brand owners.

Segments: The domestic market served by Bangkok Garment is broken into three segments: Licensed Brand (Dart), Customer Owned Brands, and Special Order. For detailed information concerning the size and characteristics of these segments see Exhibit 3 and 4.

Licensed Brand: Dart, which accounted for nearly 20% of Bangkok Garment's unit sales in the current year, is one of the best known brands of mens' shirts in Thailand. The licensor is a German firm that has been very successful at marketing and licensing this brand throughout the world. Rueng acquired the exclusive use of this brand in Thailand ten years ago, and assigned it to their marketing company Rueng World-Wide. This arrangement relieves Bangkok Garment of the expense and the responsibility of managing the retail marketing effort. One of the ways that Rueng has built the popularity of the Dart brand is through product innovation. Striped fabrics were one of these innovations. Today, striped fabrics account for well over half the retail sales of these garments in Thailand. The primary competition in this market segment comes from the owners of other licensed brands, some of whom do their own manufacturing (while others subcontract).

Because Dart is marketed in many countries, typically under the ownership of a local licensee, Bangkok Garment has been successful in becoming a Thailand source for different licensees in other countries.

Dart's world-wide reputation is significant, as nearly 30% of this brand's sales in Thailand at retail are to tourists. Tourists find that they can buy Dart shirts for approximately half of what they pay for this shirt in other countries.

In addition to manufacturing product under the Dart name and marketing them through the Rueng World-Wide organization, Bangkok garment also owns several European and American brands. This means that they are responsible for marketing and selling these products at the retail level. To date, however, these brands have accounted for only a small portion of sales in Thailand. The opportunities for growth in this area are considerable.

Customer Owned Brands: Because Bangkok Garment is largely a manufacturer, other brands have used them to produce competitive products. The company, therefore, produces products that are competitors to Dart and their own brands.

Some of these customer owned brands were started and are owned by Thailand businesses. Others are brands which are licensed in Thailand by competitors. Examples of these are Nike, Puma, Hang-Ten, Grand Slam and Didora.

Customer owned brands are currently a very small portion of Bangkok Garment's sales, but the opportunities for growth are substantial. A particularly bothersome form of competition in this segment comes from the many small garment manufacturers located throughout Thailand. They compete on the basis of price and short delivery lead times, typically placing orders for fabric with a wide variety of area suppliers.

Specials: Many Thailand companies, in a broad variety of industries, use sportswear as a customer incentive. This is done in two main ways. One way is to include a garment as part of a promotional offer, and the other is to distribute garments to customers as part of a special event. These events may be sponsored sports tournaments, company outings, or special occasions. Typically, the company purchasing garments for either of these purposes prefers solid colors that enable them to silk screen or embroider company logos or commemorative information on the item. Often the colors selected are those of the company's logo or brand.

Since these products are not sold at retail, the basis for the purchase decision is quite different from the retail purchases. Exhibit 5 shows the buying behavior for all of the domestic market segments. An advantage enjoyed by Bangkok in this particular market segment is its long standing reputation for the manufacture of high quality garments. Therefore, there is real value to a company that purchases these shirts to have the name "Bangkok Garment" on the label. Like customer brands, this segment is a relatively small portion of total sales, but the opportunities for growth are substantial. As in the case of customer owned brands, the small local competitor is capable of challenging Bangkok in this segment also.

Stock Orders: Second grade products, products made too late to ship, or licensed brand products which failed to sell at retail are referred to as "orders from stock". They are offered for sales in company stores and various exhibitions. Currently, they represent a small part of total sales and should decline in significance, due to increased quality efforts and a greater understanding of the market place.

Export Sales

The export market served by Bangkok Garment includes four main segments; Australia, Hong Kong, Japan, Scandinavia, and the U.S.

Australia: Sales to Australia are made to the local licensee of the Dart brand, a company called the Dundee Corporation. Dundee was recently acquired by a Hong Kong based firm which uses manufacturing companies from many Asian countries to produce its products. Currently, Bangkok garment produces about one-tenth of Dundee's total product requirements.. Although Bangkok Garment gained entry to Dundee because of its joint association with the Dart brand, this association has become less important since the Hong Kong acquisition. Because of improving quality, and labor costs that are approximately one-seventh of those in Thailand, manufacturers in China appear to be a real threat to this part of the business; particularly for simpler garments made from solid colors. This is of real concern since Dundee currently accounts for approximately one-third of Bangkok Garment's unit sales. Because of these competitive pressures, selling price dominates the purchase decision process (Exhibit 6).

Hong Kong: Bright Star is a Hong Kong based company which owns a large number of easily recognized international brands of apparel. These include: Arnold Palmer, Jack Nicklaus, and Fred Perry. Sales to Bright Star represent nearly 20% of Bangkok Garment's current unit sales. An attractive characteristic of sales to this company is their emphasis on product features rather than price (Exhibit 6). A concern with this company, however, is outside competition from mainland China at the lower end of their product line, and Italian firms at the higher end. Current economic conditions, combined with a favorable exchange rate, have made the Italian firms a competitive threat in the international garment market, particularly in more fashion oriented garments.

Japan: Sales to Japan are largely through a single customer, Naiiko. Naiiko owns a large number of international and Japanese brands including their own, Hideiko. Customers served by Naiiko demand higher quality than any other segment served by Bangkok Garment. Their customers also value enhancements to either the fabric or the product. It is for this reason that products sold to Japan use more silk screening and embroidery. These designs also require a higher degree of workmanship. Bangkok Garment is currently discussing the use of alternative finishing methods in fabric manufacture to improve the feel of the garment. They are also looking at the use of finer count yarns for the same purpose.

Approximately two years ago Bangkok Garment's export sales manager made a special effort to increase the sales to Japan. These efforts were successful to the point that sales in units quadrupled and now represent 10% of the total.

Scandinavia: A common problem faced by Thailand garment manufacturers is the imposition of quotas by the U.S. and many European countries. The formation of the European Economic Community (EEC) has only aggravated this problem, making it more difficult to gain access to these markets. One exception to this rule is the non-EEC Scandinavian countries (where quotas do not currently exist). This makes Scandinavia attractive as an export market.

Originally, the Scandinavian market sourced its products in continental Europe, but as the difference in cost between European and Asian manufacturers grew it found itself seeking sources of products in Asia. Due to increasing incomes, the overall market for sportswear garments is experiencing strong growth in Scandinavia. Bangkok Garment faces limited Thailand competitors. Current sales to this market segment are less that 5% of the total, but they are forecast to grow dramatically (Exhibit 3). The potential entry of Scandinavia into the EEC would, therefore, be problematic.

U.S.: There is a huge market (currently untapped) for Bangkok Garment in the U.S.. Unfortunately, it is a quota market.[3] Although the merchandising group of Bangkok Garment is less familiar with this segment (that is why no order winning criteria are shown in Exhibit 6), it is known that the U.S. market is becoming increasingly demanding concerning workmanship, product features, and product quality, i.e., requiring A to C levels of product difficulty. In addition, U.S. based customers know that they represent huge volumes for most manufacturers, and therefore demand very competitive pricing.

A recent small initial order from one of the large mass merchandisers in the U.S. has served to interest the Bangkok Garment manager in participating further in the U.S. market. An issue that Bangkok Garment will face in this market, besides that of obtaining the necessary quotas, will be choosing which customers to serve. The U.S. market has a much broader variety of retail outlets than the Thailand domestic market.

---

[3] Import quotas are characteristic of the U.S. and European markets, and are based on specific products. To export to a quota market, a company must get quota approval from the Thailand Foreign Trade Department which is a government unit. There are two types of quota. Performance quota are awarded according to the export history of a company. Central pool quota is quota that results from companies that have been unable to sell up to their quota limit, or results from trade negotiations. Quotas are increased for one to two reasons. First, countries typically provide for a small increase, e.g. 3-5% annually, to account for normal market growth. Second, on occasion the governments of Thailand and the importing country engage in trade negotiations which result in dramatic increases in quota limits. Failure of a firm to sell its entire quota to an importing country in anyone year results in the loss of quota, but the loss is triple the actual sales gap.

Therefore, this market will force Bangkok Garment to determine in which of these segments they can be most competitive.

Manufacturing

The same basic production process is used for all of the sportswear produced by Bangkok Garment. There are three basic steps in the production process: 1) marking, grading and cloth cutting, 2) sewing, and 3) finishing and packing.

Marking, Grading and Cloth Cutting: This operation begins with product specification sheets. There are important differences to consider between the manufacturing of solid color and striped sport shirts at this stage of the process.

Solid Color Fabrics: In the case of solid color fabrics, a computer based marking and grading process is used to prepare a paper pattern for cutting each component part in the garment. First, a computer wand is moved around the perimeter of each master part pattern and the exact dimensions of the piece are transmitted to a computer representation of the piece. Next, the computer pictures of the pattern parts are placed on a template of the cloth as it would be on the cutting table, graded for size, and the layout is optimized for fabric yield. Finally, a large template sheet, covering the entire table, is printed out. The individual patterns on this sheet are checked for accuracy, and the sheet is sent to the marking, grading and cutting department.

Exhibit 7 shows pictures of two steps in the computer marking and grading operation for solid color fabrics. For order sizes smaller than 400 units, this process can produce at the rate of 1600 shirts per day, and for orders exceeding 400 units approximately 5300 shirts per day can be produced.

For solid color items a team of two or three operators, depending on the order size, performs the lay-up, cutting and bundling operations. Cloth is placed on the cutting table in layers and the paper pattern is placed on top of the cloth. Next, a plastic sheet is placed over the paper pattern and a vacuum is drawn, compressing the layers of cloth. The cutting operator uses a straight knife to cut out the individual parts. For the cutting of some items, such as collar linings, a die cutting press is used.

Each garment part is numbered for identification. These parts are then separated by style, size and color, and combined into a single lot before the order is sent to the sewing section. The productivity of the cloth cutting team for lay-up, cutting and bundling is 600 shirts per day per operator (for polo shirts). For T-shirts the productivity is approximately 15% greater. Exhibit 8 shows pictures of the cloth cutting operation for solid color fabrics. Twelve people are involved in the cutting of solid fabric.

Striped Fabrics: A different marking, grading and cutting process is used in the production of shirts made from striped fabric because of the importance and difficulty of matching up the fabric stripes in assembling the final garment. This process is shown in Exhibit 9. First, the rolls of cloth are cut into small blocks and stacked in layers. Each block is for a separate component parts. Next, each part is marked and graded separately for cutting. The pattern is marked on the top piece of fabric in each block of fabric and the layers of cloth are pinned together to prevent movement. Finally, the block is cut into individual cloth pieces, using a straight knife. Some parts, however, such as small pockets, are cut using a band knife.

Teams of four to six people, depending on the style of the product, perform the work. Each team includes people designated as markers, layers, cutters, and bundlers. Marking requires much higher skill than other operations as these employees can have a very important impact on fabric yields. In total, 15 people perform the marking , grading, and the cutting of striped fabric. The productivity for the striped fabric marking, grading, cutting and bundling teams is about 100 shirts per day per operator for small stripes, and 150 shirts per day for large stripes. At times it is necessary to transfer people between the solid and stripe work groups because of workload conditions.

Sewing: The company has eight sewing lines, each line having one supervisor, one service person and one or two quality control inspectors. Three different types of sewing processes are used.

Lines 1 and 2 are used to produce complicated products, i.e. shirts having complex pocket and collar designs. These lines produce complicated export products, typically averaging in excess of 3000 shirts per day. These lines have 30 to 31 operators and require a higher skill than other sewing lines. Productivity averages 300 shirts on the first day of an order with productivity typically increasing to 400 shirts on the second day. From day three onward the productivity normally averages 500 shirts per day.

The design of line 3 is similar to lines 1 and 2, but it is normally dedicated to the production of Dart shirts for the domestic market.

Lines 4 through 6 are used to produce products having a simpler design, i.e. products having pockets and collars of standard design. Typically, these lines produce export products, such as the Dundee products for Australia, which are less complicated. These lines have 27 operators and normally produce 600 shirts per day on orders that normally average 4000 units. The set-up time for individual orders is not significant.

Lines 7 and 8 process small orders of high variety. The order sizes are normally less than 1000 units, and the set up time averages about 45 minutes. This line typically has a large number of collar/size/style changes. Twenty-eight operators are assigned to this line, producing between 300 and 400 shirts per day.

Sewing productivity is largely affected by the design of particular product features, the degree of stripe matching, and order size. Pictures of two sewing lines are shown in Exhibit 10.

Defects are higher on lines 1 through 3 than lines 4 through 6, and higher repair costs are incurred. The repair costs normally run about 10% of the direct labor cost. White fabric is especially difficult due to soiling. The production of second quality product before repairing is usually 30-39% of the production quantity. This drops to 3% after repair. Half of the defects are due to workmanship, with the remainder due to soiled fabric.

Finishing and Packing: The completed shirts are then sent from sewing to the finishing and packing department. This section employs 30 people. They wash (when required), iron, fold or hang, tag, and pack the garments. Productivity for ironing typically runs 200 shirts per day per operator for cotton fabrics, and 300-350 shirts per day per operator for polyester fabrics. The folding operation produces about 350-400 shirts per day per operator, while the packing operation is capable of producing 4000 shirts per day per operator. Pictures of these process steps are shown in Exhibit 11.

Labor Costs

Bangkok Garment pays the workforce on a daily wage basis. The daily wage depends on the skill and experience of the employee. New unskilled employees make $5.00 per day, and highly skilled employees with several years of experience make $6.00 per day. These rates do not include overtime, and all of the training provided by the company is on-the-job training.

Recently, labor turnover has been quite high. During the first seven months of the current year, the labor turnover, expressed as a percent of total employment level each month, varied from 1.7 to 4.3%, and averaged 3.2%. Labor turnover is more severe in cloth cutting than in sewing.

Product Costing

Bangkok Garment uses a standard cost system for pricing and factory performance evaluation purposes. Exhibit 7 shows a typical cost sheet for a sportswear item, and an example product is shown in Exhibit 8. Raw material costs are detailed in the upper portion of the cost sheet, and separated into three cost categories: fabric, accessories, and packaging material. Each cost is computed, considering the amount of material used, the unit price paid to suppliers, and the estimated yield from the material supplied by vendors. In addition, a 5% waste factor is assumed on all products to account for the production of defective products.

Additional costs are included in the lower portion of the cost sheet. The labor cost per unit is determined by first averaging all of the wage costs for the factory, including the salaries of the production manager, his staff, and the production employees, to determine an average daily wage cost per employee for all factory employees as shown in Exhibit 12. Next, this cost is divided by the average number of units produced per day per employee in the sewing lines in order to estimate the average labor cost per unit. This productivity factor is determined by preparing a time study of the sewing operations on the shirt.

In a similar manner, the annual costs of overhead, energy, and depreciation are divided by the number of production days per year to estimate the average cost per employee per day for each of these cost categories. These costs are, in turn, divided by the average sewing productivity, measured in units per day, and allocated on a per unit basis. All of the individual costs are then summed to estimate the total cost per unit for each product.

To determine a suggested price, administrative costs (of 9%) and profit (of 10%) are added to the factory cost per unit to determine a selling price per unit.

Recent Manufacturing Initiatives

During the past few years several investments have been made by Mr. Mana in the manufacturing process.

Computer Marking and Grading: Three years ago Bangkok invested in computer technology to permit garment patterns for solid fabrics to be produced on computer aided design equipment. This equipment, shown earlier in Exhibit 7, has enabled the company to achieve higher product yields, thereby reducing direct costs by approximately 4%. This equipment, representing an investment of $80,000, automatically marks the patterns and makes the product size variations (grading). Other benefits include a reduction in the number of skilled people needed; a lead time reduction of one to three days; improved labor productivity of approximately .0035 hours per shirt (for order sizes exceeding 400 shirts); and the enabling of direct communication with the customer's equipment.

Automated Embroidering Machine: The company has replaced some of the general purpose sewing machines with special purpose machines dedicated to a particular sewing operation such as embroidery and pocket making. The five embroidery machines represented an investment of about $80,000 each. This equipment reduced direct costs by 50%, in comparison with the previous subcontracting of this work. It also enabled production of up to seven colors, providing a product feature advantage. In addition, it reduced overall manufacturing lead time.

The computerized sewing machines for pockets represented an investment of $2000 for each of some 60 machines. This equipment provided direct labor savings, and enabled improvements in product appearance.

Silk Screening Process: A silk screening process was installed to enable the production of printed products. This represented an investment of $11,000 and provided the following benefits: improved quality, since the product samples are produced much closer to the actual production items; customer design security, since subcontracting is not required; shorter overall manufacturing lead times; and direct cost savings.

Cloth Testing Equipment: This equipment provides the means to inspect rolls of cloth as they are received from suppliers. The principal benefits include: improved product quality; direct material savings; and a reduction in the amount of second quality product produced.

Manufacturing Performance

In preparing the business strategy review, Mr. Mana developed the analysis of manufacturing performance by market segment shown in Exhibit 14. One of his concerns was the introduction of the high value products having complex features. Examples of this are those products requiring up to six color silk screen printing with large screens on solid fabric for the Japanese market. Not only is the printing operation slow, but the use of printed fabric has an unfavorable impact on productivity in the cutting operations. When non-printed fabric is used, in either solid color or striped design, the cutting operation can produce 4000 shirts per day at current staffing levels. Similar productivity can be achieved when printed designs are applied to fabric that is purchased in rolls. However, in some of the newer designs it is necessary to silk screen the printed design on individual fabric parts. This is done in the cutting operations. When this occurs, cutting operation productivity drops by 50% because of the extra operations involved. In this case, for example, direct labor per shirt can increase from .67 to 1.48 hours.

Increased customer pressure for improved product quality concerned Mr. Mana. Currently, the factory operates a 6% average quality level (AQL). However, Dundee in Australia and the new U.S. proposal calls for an AQL of 4%. Furthermore, Naiiko in Japan is pressing for a 2.5% AQL. In discussing this issue with Mr. Kittikachorn, the Factory Manager, it appeared that several changes would be needed during the next year of more to achieve the increased quality standards. They are an increase in the supervisory coverage on sewing lines; two additional quality control inspectors in each sewing line; and longer cycle times in sewing (i.e. lower factory productivity). Any reduction in factory productivity would be most difficult during periods of peak demand.

Finally, Mr. Mana noted that he expects further customer pressure for shorter delivery lead times in the export market. Recently, one customer raised the possibility of receiving delivery 45 days from time of order. Current lead times quoted by fabric suppliers vary from three to four and one-half months for solid color fabric and, four to five and one-half months for striped fabric. In addition, fabric suppliers typically require a minimum order quantity of 400 pieces per color.

44

Questions for Students

Review the market segments targeted by the company and the recent and proposed marketing initiatives.

1.   What market requirements are being placed on manufacturing?

2.   What are the characteristics of the process choice decisions made by manufacturing?

3.   How well is manufacturing performing against the market requirements placed on manufacturing?

4.   What are the important strategic issues for marketing and manufacturing?

Exhibit 1

**Bangkok Garment Company
ORGANIZATION CHART**

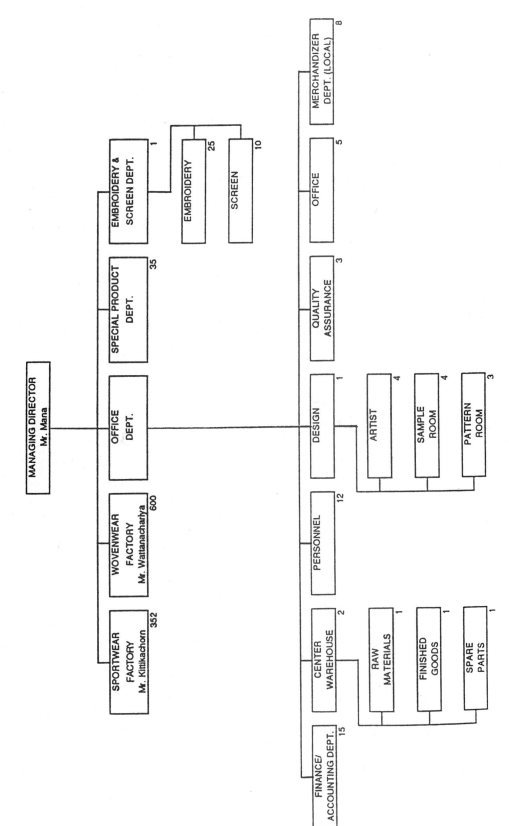

Note Number represents number of people assigned to the function.

Exhibit 2

Bangkok Garment Company
SPORTWEAR FACTORY ORGANIZATION CHART

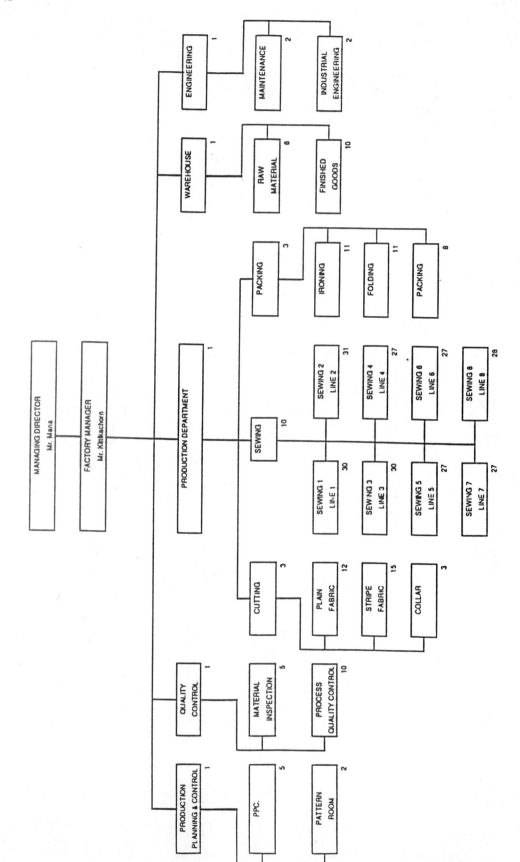

Note: Number represents number of people assigned to the function.

EXHIBIT 3

SALES ANALYSIS

MARKET SEGMENT	UNIT SALES VOLUME			
	TWO YEARS AGO	CURRENT YEAR	IN THREE YEARS	IN FIVE YEARS
EXPORT:				
UNIT —	295,920	828,777	1,008,000	1,080,000
PERCENTAGE	41	70	70	60
DUNDEE	149,508	390,084	290,000	270,000
OTHER —	146,412	438,693	718,000	810,000
SCANDANAVIA	5,256	41,664	63,121	90,000
HONG KONG	27,312	233,364	118,352	135,000
JAPAN	24,312	105,540	157,805	187,500
ITALY	–	27,252	23,670	30,000
SINGAPORE	38,220	22,368	47,341	52,500
CANADA	60	8,505	7,890	9,000
U.S.	–	–	236,703	298,500
OTHER	50,568	–	63,121	7,500
DOMESTIC:				
UNITS	424,018	349,980	430,000	720,000
PERCENTAGE	59	30	30	40
LICENSED BRAND	268,570	224,043	300,000	563,000
CUSTOMER BRAND	107,406	28,956	60,000	72,000
SPECIALS	22,512	32,988	30,000	45,000
STOCK	24,792	62,520	40,000	40,000
OTHER BANGKOK BRANDS	738	1,473	–	–
TOTAL PER YEAR	719,938	1,178,757	1,440,000	1,800,000
AVERAGE MONTHLY	59,995	100,000	120,000	150,000

EXHIBIT 4

MARKET SEGMENT ANALYSIS

	DART	OTHER BANGKOK BRANDS "A"	OTHER BANGKOK BRANDS "B"	CUSTOMER OWNED BRANDS	SPECIALS	DUNDEE	BRIGHT STAR	JAPAN	SCANDINAVIAN
SELLING PRICE/PC	$6.66	$5.40	$7.11	$7.15	6.83	$4.40	$7.34	$7.55	$8.02
PRODUCTION ORDER SIZE (PCS) (1)	1636	332	264	1256	348	3941	1582	3177	618
$CONTRIBUTION MARGIN/PC	1.00	1.87	1.28	2.61	2.48	0.49	1.34	2.34	1.19
CONTRIBUTION MARGIN % SELLING PRICE	15	35	18	37	36	11	18	31	15
FABRIC TYPE	60% 100% Cotton / 40% 50/50 Polyester Cotton	50/50 Polyester Cotton	100% Cotton	100% Cotton	83% 100% Cotton / 17% 50/50 Polyester Cotton	50/50 Polyester Cotton	100% Cotton	100% Cotton	100% Cotton
PATTERN TYPE (2)									
SOLID %	10	10		33		30	60	60	20
STRIPE %	90	90	100	67	100	70	40	40	80
DIRECT LABOR $/PC	0.68	0.41	1.23	0.67	0.63	0.57	0.49	0.54	0.48
DIRECT MATERIAL $/PC	4.98	3.12	4.60	3.87	3.72	3.34	5.51	4.67	6.37
DIRECT MATERIAL % SELLING PRICE	73	58	64	54	59	77	75	62	78
TOTAL LABOR HOURS/PC	0.46	0.4	0.75	0.47	0.41	0.41	0.44	0.48	0.42

Note   (1) Based on actual shipment quantity
            (2) Estimated by management

EXHIBIT 5

ORDER WINNING CRITERIA: BANGKOK GARMENT-DOMESTIC MARKET

	DART	OTHER BANGKOK BRANDS	CUSTOMER OWNED BRANDS	SPECIAL ORDERS	STOCK ORDERS
PRICE		Q	Q	15	20
PRICE/QUALITY RELATIONSHIP	40				
PRODUCTION FLEXIBILITY	Q	10	20	Q	
PRODUCTION CAPABILITY			50	40	
QUALITY			30		15
DELIVERY RELIABILITY			Q	40	
DELIVERY SPEED (15 DAYS)	Q			5	
PRODUCT FEATURES		60			
BRAND AWARENESS	60	30			60
PRODUCT AVAILABILITY					5

NOTES:

1. Product Features: Fabric finishing, workmanship, and design innovation.
2. Customer Owned Brands: Currently getting price premium.
3. Production Capability (in customer owned brands): Can do all operations with no subcontracting. (This provides design security for the customer.)
4. Production Capability (in specials): Reputation for Dart quality level. Flexibility in fabric type, operations, and product features.
5. Production Flexibility: Color variety, quality, design features.

EXHIBIT 6

ORDER WINNING CRITERIA: BANGKOK GARMENT--EXPORT MARKET

	JAPAN/ SCANDINAVIA	DUNDEE	BRIGHT STAR
PRICE	20	60	10
PRODUCT FEATURES	40	10	20
DELIVERY RELIABILITY	10	10	10
PRODUCTION FLEXIBILITY	30	20	60
DELIVERY SPEED			

NOTES:
1. Delivery Reliability: Allow up to one week late delivery.
2. Production Flexibility: Color variety, quantity, design features.
3. Product Features: Fabric finishing, workmanship, and design innovation.

SOLID COLOR FABRIC: MARKING AND GRADING OPERATIONS

Reading the Pattern Dimensions into the Computer:

Optimizing the Template Layout:

EXHIBIT 8

SOLID COLOR FABRIC: CUTTING OPERATIONS

Template and Fabric Ready for Cloth Cutting:

Cut Parts:

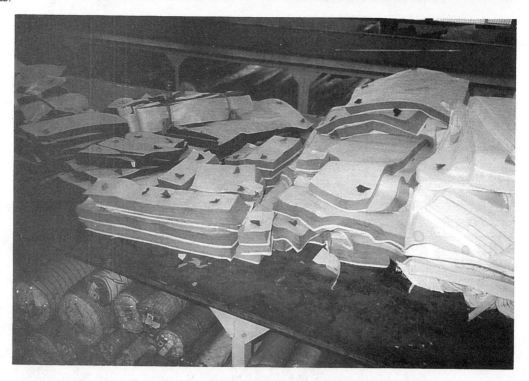

STRIPED FABRIC FOR MARKING, GRADING, AND CUTTING OPERATIONS

Marking the Blocks for Cutting:

Cutting the Fabric Parts:

EXHIBIT 10

SEWING OPERATION

Sewing Line 1:

Sewing Line 4:

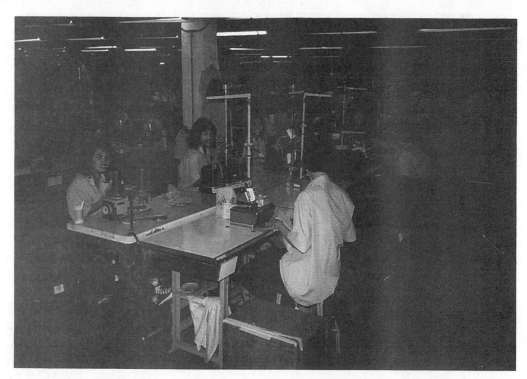

FINISHING AND PACKING OPERATIONS

Ironing and Folding the Shirts:

Packing the Shirts:

EXHIBIT 12

BANGKOK GARMENT COMPANY
COST SHEET: STYLE NUMBER 1234
100% COTTON
SOLID COLOR

DESCRIPTION	UNIT COST
Fabric:	
Body Fabric	$4.010
Placket	0.104
Neck Band	0.047
Placket Lining	0.011
Waste (at 5%)	0.209
Sub-Total	4.381
Accessories:	
Thread: Body	0.033
Texture	0.030
Size Label	0.017
Tape	0.002
Button	0.014
Logo Tape	0.200
Other	0.080
Waste (at 5%)	0.019
Sub-Total	0.395
Packing	
Poly Bag	0.024
Card Board	0.022
Clip	0.007
Fins	0.003
Other	0.040
Waste (at 5%)	0.005
Box	0.015
Sub-Total	0.116
Total Raw Material	4.892
Capacity/Day/Person	17

	Cost/Day/Person	Percent	Total
Raw Materials		89.42	$4.89
Labor Cost	$8.240	8.37	0.46
Overhead	1.068	1.08	0.06
Energy	0.346	0.35	0.02
Depreciation	0.768	0.78	0.04
Total Cost		100.00	5.47
Administration (at 9%)			0.49
Profit (at 10%)			0.55
Suggested Price			$6.51

Exhibit 13

Example Product

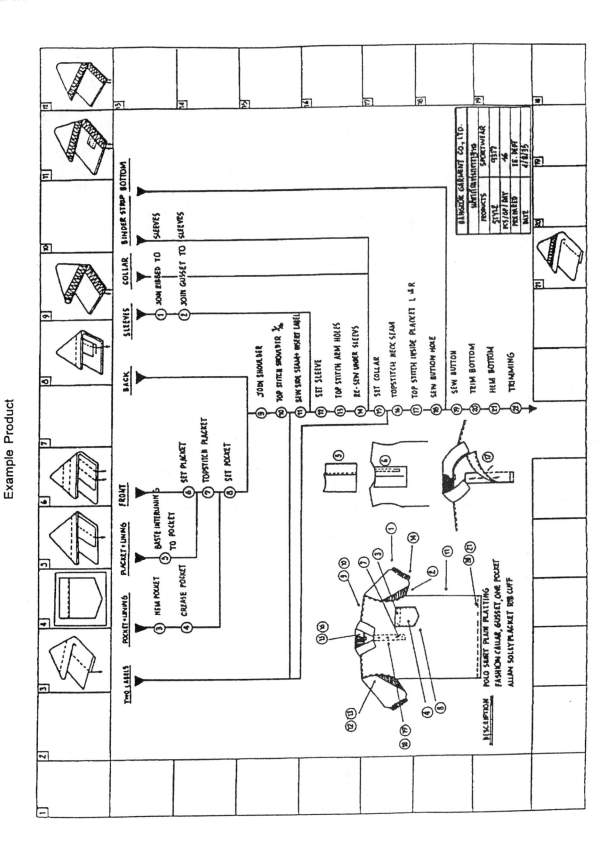

EXHIBIT 14

MARKET SEGMENT ANALYSIS—MANUFACTURING PERFORMANCE

		OTHER BANGKOK BRANDS							
	DART	"A"	"B"	CUSTOMER OWNED BRANDS	SPECIALS	DUNDEE	BRIGHT STAR	JAPAN	SCANDINAVIAN
PRODUCT DIFFICULTY CODE (1)									
A	80%	--	50%	17%	--	--	--	10%	20%
B	20%	--	50%	50%	--	8%	--	40%	60%
C	--	100%	--	33%	83%	54%	100%	50%	20%
D	--	--	--	--	--	30%	--	--	--
E	--	--	--	--	17%	8%	--	--	--
AVERAGE \$CONTRIBUTION MARGIN/ SEWING LINE HOUR (2)									
LINES 1-3	\$49.04	\$74.44		\$114.58	\$118.39	\$47.17	\$86.11	\$133.64	\$60.55
LINES 4-6	\$47.17		49.84	\$153.75		\$33.00	\$82.50		\$43.19
LINES 7-8				\$125.43	\$98.10				
ACTUAL LEAD TIME (DAYS)									
SOLID	194	86	110	123	68	109	190	230	165
STRIPED	194			167		155	211	227	197
DELIVERY RELIABILITY (DAYS)									
SOLID	73	-1	0	11	0	9	1	5	18
STRIPED	73			10		12	19	-7	19

Notes:

1. Product Difficulty Code A refers to the more complicated products requiring higher employee skills, and E refers to the least complicated products to manufacture requiring less skilled employees.

2. The \$contribution margin per sewing line hour is computed by dividing the unit \$contribution margin by the sewing line hours per unit. The \$contribution margin is based on actual shipping quantities. For example, in the case of Bangkok Brand A:

$$\text{Total Hours per Lot} = \text{Setup Time plus Run Time}$$
$$= .75 \text{ hrs} + \text{Average Lot Size} \times \text{Run Time per/pc.}$$
$$= .75 + 332 \,(8 \text{ hours}/350 \text{ pcs}) = 8.34 \text{ hours}$$

$$\text{Total Hours per Unit} = 8.34/332 = .02512 \text{ hours}$$
$$\text{\$Contribution per Sewing Hour} = \$1.87/.0251 = \$74.44$$

Case 1.5

COLGATE-PALMOLIVE HUNGARY

Summary

"Colgate-Palmolive Hungary" was written to provide a basis for discussion on the challenges facing a rapidly growing subsidiary in the midst of a turbulent political, economic and organizational environment. The parent company, a global consumer products firm experiencing severe competition in the U.S., is looking increasingly to the European and Asian markets to boost its margins. Meanwhile, management at the Hungarian subsidiary must respond strategically to continuing growth in an environment of uncertain economics, changing politics and increasing competition. Internally, the company faces logistical and organizational structure issues. The myriad of challenges facing the company provides a comprehensive case study for the student of strategic management.

PARENT COMPANY BACKGROUND

Colgate-Palmolive, headquartered in New York City, is the world's leading manufacturer of oral care products, with more than 40 percent of the global market share in toothpaste, and the leading seller of liquid soaps in the U.S. and worldwide. Both product lines are marketed under the company's own name. Deriving 65 percent of its sales from outside the U.S. and Canada, the company has operations in 75 countries and exports products to 100 others. The U.S. retail environment has become increasingly competitive, exacerbated by the consumer trend towards non-brand name or generic consumer goods. Retailers have not discouraged this trend, since store brands typically mean higher profit margins. Colgate is responding to the difficult and competitive U.S. retail environment through global expansion and new product introduction [6].

With its 266 manufacturing, office, distribution, and research facilities worldwide, Colgate-Palmolive has the ability and resources to respond rapidly to changing global trends. The company has come to recognize the importance of the market potential of newly industrializing countries and has initiated, or expanded, operations in such countries as Cambodia, Bulgaria, Tanzania, and Hungary. According to Al Ries, the chairman of a marketing strategy firm, brand equity may be suffering in the U.S., but other countries look to American brands, which can often command premiums over those made by inferior local competitors [6].

One of the competitive advantages of Colgate internationally is its "bundle book" which contains all the information a Colgate country manager needs to know about a product, including the product attributes and manufacturing formula, standards for packaging, relevant market research and the points that need to be made in advertising. The book creates uniformity of products worldwide and provides a broad strategy for the company's country managers; specific organizational issues, however, typically are left up to the managers [3].

This case was prepared by Professor Mzamo P. Mangaliso, University of Massachusetts, Amherst, Priti R. Patel, and Jann-Marie Halvorsen for class discussion and does not necessarily imply either good or poor managment practices.

Company History

The Colgate-Palmolive Company was formed in 1928 as the result of a merger between the Colgate Company of Jersey City, NJ (a consumer product firm founded in 1806) and the Palmolive Company of Milwaukee, WI (a soap manufacturer founded in 1864 as the B.B. Johnson Soap Company). During the 1930s the company purchased French and German soap makers and opened its first branches in Europe. Post-World War II, the Ajax, Colgate, and Palmolive brands were outselling the European competition. The company expanded to the Far East in the 1950s, and by 1961 foreign sales represented 52% of the total.

During the 1960s and 1970s, the company diversified by buying approximately 70 other companies. This diversification strategy, however, proved unsuccessful and Colgate divested itself of most of these companies during the 1980s. The man behind the divestitures was Reuben Mark, who spent his entire career at Colgate and became chief executive in 1984. That year, Colgate's gross margins were just over 39 percent, but by 1993 they had increased to nearly 48 percent. Operating margins more than doubled between 1984 and 1992. The company's financial success over this time period was attributed to Mark's cost-cutting efforts, focus on core businesses with a move towards the higher-margin personal care products, strategic acquisitions within the core businesses and attention to detail.

In 1987, when Mark launched a reorganization to focus on building Colgate-Palmolive's core businesses (personal care and household products), the company took a $145 million charge against earnings to cover reorganization costs. From 1986 to 1991, the company introduced three new products and acquired eight companies worldwide. In 1991 the company took a one-time $243 million charge to simplify and consolidate global production facilities to capitalize on falling trade barriers. Mark closed or reengineered a number of the company's worldwide plants and by 1993 had brought the number down from 156 to 80. The 1991 restructuring also included reducing the 42,800 worldwide employment force by 20,000. To avoid firing a disproportionate number of minorities or those close to retirement, Mark insisted that he approve all layoff lists [3].

In the second quarter of 1994, the company experienced problems in the U.S. Although worldwide, the unit sales volume was up nine percent and earnings per share were up 13 percent, the figures belied the North American results of a nine percent unit sales decline in the soap, detergent and toothpaste businesses which resulted in a 13 percent decline in U.S. revenues. Mark denied rumors of another major restructuring and instead launched a number of new products in oral and personal care and invested in substantial advertising in the U.S. market [5].

BACKGROUND ON HUNGARY

Hungary is an Eastern European country with a population of 10.5 million people. Approximately 58 percent of the population live in urban areas (approximately 2 million in Budapest alone) with the remaining 42 percent residing in the rural regions. The purchasing power of the majority of Hungarians is low compared to Western European standards. For example, it takes the average Hungarian 1.6 hours of work to buy one 75ml tube of Colgate toothpaste, compared to 12 minutes of work for the average German worker.

Despite Hungary's tradition of private ownership under communism, the transition to a market economy is proving difficult. Only about 10% of communist-era enterprises have been privatized. Although Hungary leads Eastern Europe in foreign investment (60% of joint ventures are with German and Austrian companies) with about $3 billion in direct investment, there have been some problems in making these ventures profitable (e.g., GE/Tungsram) and some cultural conflicts (such as Suzuki's attempt to impose Japanese management methods). On the positive side, private ownership in services is growing quickly and in some fields, such as tourism, is replacing state ownership. Hungary is the most systematic of the Eastern European countries in its attempts to attract foreign capital; banking regulations are being adapted and privatization provisions formulated to facilitate international investors [4].

The economy of the country has been threatened by Hungary's need to buy oil on the world markets rather than through barter with the Soviet Union as was done prior to the fall of communism. Following the outbreak of war in Yugoslavia, the unemployment conditions worsened in Hungary with the influx of thousands of Yugoslavian refugees, many with Hungarian family ties. In April of 1992, the Hungarian unemployment rate stood at 9 percent; it peaked in 1993 at 14 percent and by July 1994, was hovering at approximately 12 percent (versus an average 14 percent for Eastern Europe overall and just above 10 percent for Western Europe) [1]. Hungary's inflation rate for 1994 was 20 percent and, although high by Western standards, was down from 35 percent in 1991 [2]. Despite its economic woes, the nation enjoys one of Eastern Europe's most effective governments and has become a member of the Council of Europe.

According to Boston Consulting Group's John Lindquist, most Hungarian companies are poorly managed and structured and suffer from lack of product focus, excessive levels of vertical integration, underdeveloped sales and distribution networks, poor labor productivity, inefficient use of resources, inflexible and overly functional organizational structures and a lack of management and worker incentives [4].

THE HUNGARIAN SUBSIDIARY

In 1991, Colgate-Palmolive established its Hungarian subsidiary in Budapest, with an initial investment of $0.5 million, to focus on the marketing and sales of Colgate products imported as finished goods from other European subsidiaries. In 1994, Colgate invested an additional $2.0 million by acquiring a local manufacturer (Fabulon) with a plant located in the small town of Dorog, approximately 45 kilometers from Budapest. Colgate Palmolive (C-P) Hungary also owns one warehouse in Dorog and leases another in a town near Budapest.

The management at C-P Hungary has targeted three primary objectives to be attained within the next three years: (1) to have C-P Hungary become the best consumer products company in Hungary by year-end 1995, which requires becoming number one or two in the key product categories chosen for investment in the near future; (2) to run a financially healthy and growth-oriented business; and (3) to develop an exciting organization and raise the quality of each function to at least the same level as a comparable subsidiary in Western Europe. The resolution of several issues has been identified as critical to the achievement of the stated objectives. The areas of concern include the competitive environment, external market dynamics, logistics (including the Dorog facility, purchasing, and inventory control), and organizational structure.

COMPETITION

The competition in the consumer products industry in Hungary is very high, with little room for penetration and very low brand loyalty. C-P Hungary's major competitors are Proctor & Gamble, Unilever, and Henkel, all of which have larger operations and investments in Hungary than Colgate does. Proctor & Gamble began its Hungarian operation in January of 1991 with an investment of $12 million. The company concentrated in manufacturing and sales and established joint ventures in toothpaste filling and diapers. Proctor & Gamble's main product lines include detergents, oral care, pampers, and body care. Unilever began its operations in Hungary in November of 1991 with an acquisition of a local company and an investment of $49 million. The company manufactures its own detergents and liquids, soap, and margarine and butter; product-line focus is on margarine, detergent, toothpaste, body care, and ice cream. The final major competitor is Henkel which began its operations in Hungary in 1988 with several joint ventures in detergents, industrial cleaning, glue, and shoe polish. The company's investment in Hungary totals $30 million with a focus on detergents, hard surface care, body care, and glue.

MARKET DYNAMICS

Three major market occurrences are impacting C-P Hungary's business: (1) In the consumer products industry, competitive pressures are necessitating significant increases in advertising budgets; (2) political turbulence continues throughout the industry as the result of the May, 1994 election of a new socialist government; and (3) bureaucracy remains an issue, as C-P Hungary is faced with time-consuming import limitations.

LOGISTICAL ISSUES

The Dorog Facility

With the acquisition of Fabulon, C-P Hungary inherited a manufacturing plant in Dorog. The plant is well equipped for filling liquids (e.g., after-shave, gels). The Plant management objectives include optimizing investment, developing the facility's flexibility to accommodate low-volume and short-run production, and building on the strength of the present operation by optimizing equipment and developing the workers.

Purchasing

Currently, approximately 70 percent of C-P Hungary's sales are from sourcing finished products from sister subsidiaries. There are existing company guidelines that each subsidiary must follow. Each subsidiary has an appointed Inter-Company Coordinator (ICC). In the Hungarian subsidiary, the ICC is responsible for arranging for the timely supply of finished products to C-P Hungary distribution warehouses for those products which are imported. This individual is also responsible for keeping costs low, maintaining high quality, assuring the quickest delivery possible and maintaining an organized level of paperwork. C-P Hungary has one person running the finished goods purchasing department. Little or no documentation on policy and procedure on purchasing goods exists. A preliminary Inter-Company Purchasing Policy was developed but no follow-up was completed. This lack of proper documentation and total dependence on one individual poses a threat to C-P Hungary with 70 percent of its business coming from imported finished goods.

Inventory

High levels of safety stock and a high variability between forecasts and actual sales have resulted in unacceptably high levels of inventory for C-P Hungary. There are no sales forecasting systems in place and relatively little historical data available. The inventory problem has been exacerbated by a lack of proper communication among the relevant departments.

ORGANIZATIONAL STRUCTURE

The structure of the organization is in the developmental stage. There has been a recent reorganization of key people and the creation of a new department--the Human Resources Department. Five major departments report to the General Manager: Human Resources, General Administration, Finance, Marketing/Sales, and Manufacturing. Only one person handles the Human Resources Department and reports directly to the General Manager. The General Administration Department consists of an executive assistant, executive secretary and a messenger. The Finance Department is headed by the Finance Director who has reporting to him the Assistant Financial Controller, the MIS Manager and the Batch Accountant. Seven additional positions report to the Assistant Financial Controller. The financial processes and required reports are ill defined and fixed costs are not well managed. The Commercial Director (Marketing/Sales Department) has six individuals reporting to him: four Category Managers, one for each of the key product categories (oral care, body care, hard surface care/facial care, and Fabulon), a National Sales Manager and a Sales Assistant. The National Sales Manager in turn has two Sales Administrators and three Area Managers reporting to him. Three account salespeople, twelve salespeople, and twelve junior salespeople report to the three area managers. The Manufacturing Department is in the process of being developed, with plans for a Director. Once a Manufacturing Director is in place, an organizational chart for the manufacturing operation will be drawn up and the Dorog facility issues addressed.

REFERENCES

[1] *The Economist* (1994) . Out of Work in Eastern Europe. July 9: 48.

[2] *Euromoney World Economies Handbook* (1992): 80.

[3] Kindel, S.(1993). The Bundle Book. *Financial World*. January 5: 34-35.

[4] *Mergers & Acquisitions* (1991). Hungary: Advanced Outpost for a Free-Market System. March/April: 75-76.

[5] Sasseen, J. & Schiller, Z. (1994). For Colgate-Palmolive, It's Time for Trench Warfare. Business Week. September 19: 56-57.

64

[6] Sellers, P. (1993). Brands. It's Thrive or Die. *Fortune*. August 23: 52-56.

Questions for students

1. How should operations at the Dorog facility be optimized? How will purchasing and inventory be impacted?

2. Construct an organizational chart reflecting the current C-P Hungary organization. Make any recommended alternatives or modifications, along with a rationale supporting these recommendations.

3. Summarize the strengths, weaknesses, opportunities and threats facing C-P Hungary.

4. Taking the current environment into consideration, devise a creative strategic plan for the perplexing problems facing the company.

Case 1.6

Mercedes-Benz Mexico, S.A. de C.V.

Summary

Mercedes-Benz entered the Mexican market much later than other American auto companies. The Mercedes case shows how a gradual entry with a joint venture partner can allow a foreign firm to learn about an emerging market, while at the same time adjusting to constant change in the political and economic environment. Mercedes has based its market entry on a reputation for quality that is its hallmark. But changes in its external environment caused by NAFTA and the devaluation of the peso may lead Mercedes to adopt a somewhat modified strategy.

Mercedes-Benz entered the Mexican commercial automotive market in 1985. After establishing presence in this market, Mercedes began producing passenger cars. Mercedes employs a common production policy for its commercial vehicles and passenger cars in Mexico, characterized by low volumes and low automation, incremental investments and capacity increases, and parts supplied mainly through imports. Whereas commercial vehicles target both domestic and export markets, passenger cars are produced exclusively for the domestic market.

Nineteen ninety-five is a good time for Mercedes to reconsider its Mexican strategy. The devaluation of the peso last December 20, 1994 showed that producing mainly for the local market and importing a majority of the parts is an undiversified, risky strategy in an emerging market. Should Mercedes stay with this strategy to protect its brand image? Or should the company revise the strategy toward a more aggressive, export-oriented investment strategy?

Automotive Industry in Mexico

The Mexican automotive industry entered a period of change in 1983 with the relaxation of local content and foreign ownership rules through liberalization. Before the liberalization, strict rules limited foreign ownership in the industry to 49%. Imports of commercial and passenger vehicles were virtually prevented by the government with rules, regulations, and high tariff and non-tariff barriers. The aim of this protectionist government policy was to reduce dependence on imports and create a domestic automotive industry, which would in turn help drive the country's economy.

The protectionist policy led to the proliferation of a domestic automotive and auto parts industry. Despite regulations, there was also foreign direct investment in the industry aimed at the local market. For example Ford, Chrysler, General Motors, Nissan, Volkswagen, Kenworth, and Dodge have participated in the Mexican auto industry for a long period of time.

This case was written by Pelin Karakas and Ivon Wajong, MBA students in 1995 in the Max M. Fisher College of Business, The Ohio State University, under the supervision of Professors Roberto Garcia, Stephen Hills, and G. Keong Leong. This case was written for class discussion and does not necessarily imply good or poor management practices.

On the other hand, protectionist policies created a low quality, low technology industry that was inward-focused and not competitive with international standards. The liberalization that started gradually in 1983 and gained full speed with "The Decree of the Development and Modernization of the Automotive Industry" on December 11, 1989, was aimed at creating a new Mexican auto industry able to contribute to the economy through exports.

The 1989 decree includes two parts. The first part is the Automotive Decree which includes passenger cars and light and medium trucks. With this decree, passenger cars and trucks would be imported for the first time in decades, although with some restrictions, and foreigners could obtain majority ownership in this sector. The second part is the Autotransports Decree which includes heavy trucks, truck tractors, and buses. Almost all restrictions were lifted for local content and imported units on autotransport vehicles. Further liberalization of the industry would be realized with the elimination of tariff and non-tariff barriers in North America. Under the North American Free Trade Agreement (NAFTA), all tariffs in the industry would gradually be removed (through a 10-year transition period) for passenger cars and light trucks (five years for autotransport vehicles).

Apart from the tariff liberalization, three types of non-tariff barriers were gradually eliminated under NAFTA. These include trade-balancing requirements (compensation for imports to avoid large trade deficits), minimum Mexican-content rules, and limitations on foreign investment in the Mexican auto-parts industry.

Historically, the Mexican automotive industry's efficiency and competitiveness have been hurt by four factors. First, by international standards, the output of the Mexican automotive industry is relatively small. For example, in 1990, when production and sales achieved new records, only 820,000 vehicles were sold (see Exhibit 1). Size prevents assemblers from achieving economies of scale to enable them to produce cars and trucks more efficiently, and at competitive international prices.

Second, Mexican plants frequently produce a greater diversity of models than plants abroad. For example, while it is normal to limit production to two models per plant in Japan and the USA, in Mexico the number is sometimes as high as six. This increases complexity and reduces productivity.

Third, the continued existence of non-tariff barriers has prevented vehicle manufacturers from integrating Mexican operations into their global production plans. Limits on imports (restricted to 15% of domestic passenger car sales in 1991), export performance requirements, and limitations on ownership have raised the cost of producing vehicles in Mexico. Finally, lack of competition due to protectionist policies has led to poor quality in both the auto assembly and parts industry.

Increased foreign competition as a result of the liberalization policy caught many parts producers unprepared. Producers struggled to restructure their businesses and improve quality to remain competitive. Change will force some manufacturers from the market, while those that remain will be "world class" manufacturers.

Despite these obstacles, the industry has experienced rapid growth, and assemblers can now obtain the economies of scale and develop capabilities needed to produce to world class standards. The tariff liberalization measures and the systematic dismantling of Mexico's non-tariff barriers suggest that there will be tremendous bilateral trade and investment surges over NAFTA's 10-year transition period. Mexico will certainly become the target of new investment and imports from the US and other countries.

Daimler-Benz

Daimler-Benz AG was formed in Germany in 1926 from the amalgamation of DMG (Daimler-Motoren-Gesellschaft) and Benz & Cie. It has been a major automobile manufacturer in the world since then, except for a brief halt in production during World War II.

Daimler Benz is a holding company with total sales of DM 99,549 billion in 1994. Mercedes-Benz motor vehicles still form the core of Daimler-Benz. Its two divisions, Passenger Cars and Commercial Vehicles contribute approximately two-thirds of the group's overall sales.

Mercedes-Benz is the world s largest producer of trucks over six tons and the leading builder of busses from eight tons upwards. In commercial vehicles, Mercedes-Benz employs a multi-domestic strategy of producing in several countries and exporting from all these production sites. Mercedes has 32 manufacturing plants and 22 assembly plants worldwide, and owns Freightliner, a US truck manufacturer. These plants all engage in international import and export, leveraging the image "Made by Mercedes-Benz."

Mercedes-Benz is also the world's biggest name in luxury car production. Passenger cars constitute 60% of its sales. Mercedes-Benz employs a traditional strategy of exporting fully-assembled passenger cars from Germany, reinforcing the image "Made in Germany." Mercedes has assembly operations in Thailand, South Africa, Indonesia, and Mexico, but all production in these facilities are for the home markets.

One of Daimler-Benz's major subsidiaries is in Mexico. Investing in Mexico has been attractive for several reasons. First, Mexico provides a large domestic market (80 million people) and a very young population. Second, bilateral free trade agreements are opening markets to the North and the South of Mexico, and Mercedes anticipates future exports to these new markets. Finally, production costs are increasing rapidly in Germany, due to wage rate increases bargained between the German Auto Manufacturers Employers Association and the German Metalworkers Union. The prospect of shifting output to Mexico provides bargaining power for Daimler-Benz in Germany.

Entry into the Commercial Vehicle Market in Mexico

In 1985, Daimler-Benz bought 49% of a Mexican truck maker called Fabricas Autocar Mexicana (Famsa). Previously, Famsa was 100% owned by Grupo Hermes, one of the leading Mexican business groups known to have good relations with the government. Famsa had a 15% market share in the Mexican truck market. With the joint venture, Famsa started assembling Mercedes-Benz diesel engines.

In 1989, Daimler-Benz increased its share in Famsa to 80%. Mercedes-Benz took over a Grupo Hermes factory in Santiago de Tianguistenco and invested $50 million to modernize it. The product line of the "new" factory included heavy trucks, tractor trucks, and diesel engines. In 1991, Mercedes-Benz Mexico, S.A. de C.V. was founded.

There are three important reasons for forming a joint venture with a local company as an entry strategy. First, Mercedes wanted to enter the market gradually. Initially, only diesel engines were introduced. The share in the partnership was increased after the favorable reaction of the market to the engines. Subsequently, trucks were introduced. Second, by buying Famsa instead of starting a brand new operation, Mercedes purchased market share and a dealer network. Third, Grupo Hermes has good networks and government relationships, which helped in getting import licenses and overcoming the Mexican bureaucracy. Keeping the local partner (with a 20% share) even after entry ensured continuing good relations with the government. In Mexican business, networks and relationships are very important, and therefore most foreign companies prefer to have a local partner.

In October 1992, Mercedes became the number one truck producer in Mexico with a 36% share of the domestic market. Its main competitors in trucks are Dina, Kenmex, and Dodge. Dina, a national truck producer, had been the market's leader, but lost market share with the liberalization of the automotive industry and the entry of Mercedes. Kenmex is the Mexican subsidiary of Kenworth, and has a very good customer base for its tractors in Mexico.

Mercedes-Benz found it easy to gain market share in trucks. Competitors do not offer the same type of vehicle, so Mercedes trucks are very well received. It is a Brazilian type of truck as opposed to a US type and better suited for Mexican road conditions and infrastructure. The engine's reputation for quality and long life is a major factor in its success. Due to its reputation, the Mercedes truck has important marketing advantage and it is able to sell the trucks at premium prices.

On February 23, 1993, Mercedes announced that the company would build a second assembly plant in Monterrey. A vacant machine tool plant was converted and bus production began in August 1993. Mercedes-Benz Omnibuses was founded as a joint venture between Mercedes-Benz Mexico and CAIO. The cost of the factory was about $100 million. The factory has a capacity of 2,000 buses a year, with a product line that includes urban, suburban, and integral buses.

The reason for starting bus production was high demand for Mercedes buses previously imported from Brazil. It took 10 months from the purchase of the facility to the production of the first bus. If Mercedes had built the plant from scratch, it would have taken 18 months. There was pressure to start local production as soon as possible since the Mexican government was opposed to the import of large numbers of luxury buses from Brazil.

As a result of the maquiladora operations and the strong Mexican industrial base in the area, Monterrey has a good labor and supplier base and a good infrastructure. Mercedes found government support and cheap facilities in Monterrey. Monterrey is also close to the US border, allowing for easy export of vehicles to the US.

With both its bus and truck lines, Mercedes became the major player in the Mexican commercial vehicle market. This is a result of its strategy to gain market share by using the Mercedes name and quality as leverage in a relatively unexploited market. Financial and operating figures related to the market share of Mercedes-Benz Mexico are included in Exhibit 2. Chart 1 shows sales in new pesos (N$). Chart 2 shows the total investment made by Mercedes-Benz in US dollars. Chart 3 shows market share in the commercial vehicles industry.

Entry into Passenger Car Market in Mexico

In July 1989, Mercedes decided to assemble cars in Mexico with initial production targeted for the local market. It was announced that the possibility of exporting passenger cars from Mexico to the US would also be studied. This represented a big shift in Mercedes-Benz's traditional passenger car strategy.

Mercedes began its passenger car program in Mexico in 1992 by importing its E-Class mid-sized models to the country. Although only local car makers were permitted to import into Mexico at that time, permission to import the cars was granted in exchange for Mercedes' commitment to expand commercial vehicle production in Santiago to include a new small-chassis bus.

Immediately following its entry, Mercedes became the trend and market leader in the luxury car segment. Direct competition for Mercedes in Mexico is expected to come from BMW, which has recently announced its upcoming entry into the market. Other car manufacturers such as Chrysler, Ford, Volkswagen, and Nissan are not in direct competition with Mercedes in the luxury automobile market.

In May 1993, Mercedes began assembling mid-range 400E models in Mexico from semi-knockdown units with an annual capacity of 1,000 cars a year. Part of the truck plant in Santiago de Tianguistenco was converted for semi-knockdown car production with a $30 million investment. In the knock-down procedure, the body, parts, and accessories are imported from Stuttgart, Germany. The vehicle is then assembled in Mexico.

The C-Class is the most recent line of Mercedes-Benz passenger cars, and it is the first line to include a compact-size, non-luxury-class car, currently a best-seller in Europe. In early 1994, Mercedes looked at plans to build a new passenger car manufacturing plant in Monterrey, adjacent to the bus factory, where the C-Class cars would be produced. In this factory, the local content in the C-Class cars would be gradually increased to 65% so that the cars could be exported under NAFTA (without tariffs). The plan to build the factory was later dropped due to the perception that Americans still prefer the "Made in Germany" label. Mercedes felt that the American market was not yet ready for Mercedes imports made in Mexico.

On February 22, 1994, it was announced that Mercedes-Benz would start assembling its compact C-Class sedans in Santiago de Tianguistenco in the fall of that year. C-Class production began in November. The plan was to produce 1,000 cars for the local market in 1995, increasing output to 2,000 cars in 1996.

Operations in Santiago de Tianguistenco

The plant in Santiago is characterized by low volume, low automation, and low local content. The capacity is 30 engines per day in the engine plant, 15,000 trucks per year in the truck assembly plant, and 1,200 cars per year in the car assembly plant (with a planned increase to 2,000 units). The low volumes do not justify a high level of automation, and some of the conveyors in the engine plant are manual as well. Engines and passenger cars are manually painted. To maintain high quality standards, Mercedes has invested considerably in car paint rework.

Labor is a major factor in Mercedes' operations in Mexico. Although Mercedes provides intensive training for its workforce in Mexico, it does not expect to reach the same level of workforce training and experience as in Germany. Thus, labor provides a competitive advantage for operations in Mexico. As a result, Mercedes' manufacturing strategy places less emphasis on automation or advanced manufacturing technologies.

The majority of parts and supplies shipped by Mercedes to Santiago are importes. Local content is low in the final products of the Santiago plants. The engine plant is strictly an assembly operation. Eighty percent of the parts come from Brazil, where Mercedes-Benz has an established production facility and supplier base. Fifteen percent of the parts come from Germany, and only 5% are supplied from Mexico.

In trucks, local content is the highest with 50%. The chassis is 90% made in Mexico. Freightliners are also assembled in Santiago for the US market under a plan to increase the local content to 65%, and thus take advantage of NAFTA provisions in the long run. On the other hand, in car production most parts are imported and then assembled in Santiago.

Although the policy of importing a majority of the parts protects its quality image, it forces the company to face considerable currency risk. Under normal conditions, this could be managed but an unexpected event at the end of 1994 created numerous problems for the company.

Devaluation

On December 20, 1994, the Mexican peso was devalued. The extent of the devaluation took the Mexican business community by surprise. The government took measures to prevent rapid inflation. Auto manufacturers pledged to increase prices by only 10%, the rate set by government for other domestically-produced goods. This meant that producers would absorb much of the devaluation effects since by March, 1995, the Peso had lost 40% of its previous value.

Although the devaluation was expected to boost auto exports, domestic demand fell dramatically and affected car producers serving the domestic market. National demand for imported vehicles in 1995 was expected to fall from the 1994 level of 80,000 to pre-NAFTA levels of only a few thousand units per year. New truck sales fell by 86% and bus sales fell by 66% in January 1995, compared to sales in the same period of the previous year.

On January 4, Mercedes-Benz suspended production at its assembly plants in Mexico for approximately three weeks because of the currency crisis. It planned to use the temporary shut-down to clear inventory. This was followed by announcements of temporary closings of the factories of Ford, Volkswagen, and the Mexican bus and truck manufacturer Grupo Dina.

The Mercedes plants began working again on January 31. In February, advertising and publicity expenses were cut dramatically, investment decisions were postponed, one-third of the staff was laid off, and the workload was reduced to four days per week. Truck production in Santiago fell to 4,500 units per year. In the car assembly, the production plan of 1300 units for 1995 was revised to the 1994 level of 800 units. Mercedes announced that it would contract with a larger number of Mexican suppliers to take advantage of cheaper Mexican auto parts.

Mercedes, along with other manufacturers, was deeply affected by the devaluation. Its heavy imports of parts and limited exports of finished products made the company vulnerable in the current economic situation. Although Mercedes exports to Brazil and Venezuela created a natural hedge against the falling peso, they were not enough to cover losses from imports and decreases in local demand.

Future Plan

With the weak peso and a Mexican economy in recession, Mercedes has experienced the risks of producing mainly for the local market with a large proportion of imported parts. One alternative to minimize the impact of currency fluctuation is to source more parts locally. The question is whether Mercedes can find local manufacturers to produce parts that will meet its strict quality standards.

With NAFTA, a viable long-term strategy for Mercedes is to export products made in Mexico to North America. However, local content must be at least 65% which could pose quality and image problems for Mercedes. Mercedes looked into a proposal to build an export-oriented auto production facility in Monterrey in early 1994. The proposal was ultimately rejected for fear that US customers were not ready to purchase cars produced by Mercedes in Mexico. Another avenue Mercedes can pursue is to expand exports to other Latin American countries from Mexico.

Mercedes has an important stake in Mexico. In a short period of time, it has built significant market share in the commercial vehicle and luxury auto market. However, it currently faces a declining economy brought about by the falling peso. The challenge for Mercedes is to craft a strategy to weather the uncertainties of the business environment and enhance its competitive position in Mexico.

Questions for students

1. Contrast the experience of Mercedes-Benz with that of Ford (case 1.7) in adjusting to the recession of 1995.

2. Are Mercedes' differences from Ford such that it occupies a unique market niche? If so, what kind of market niche is it?

3. What does the Mercedes experience tell you about the risks and opportunities of adopting a niche market strategy?

EXHIBIT 1 : Mexican Motor Vehicle Market

Mexican Vehicle Production and Sales (1981-1992)

Year	Production	Total Sales	Domestic	Exports
1992	1,083,091	1,090,288	706,914	383,374
1991	989,373	992,276	633,610	358,666
1990	820,576	821,798	544,939	276,859
1989	641,281	641,863	445,864	195,999
1988	512,776	515,066	341,919	173,147
1983	285,485	295,271	272,815	22,456
1981	597,118	585,441	571,013	14,428

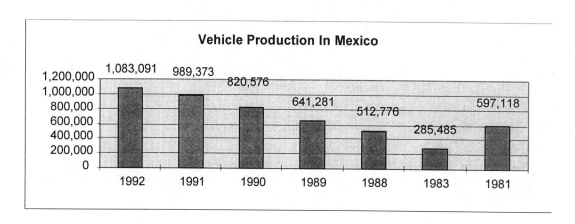

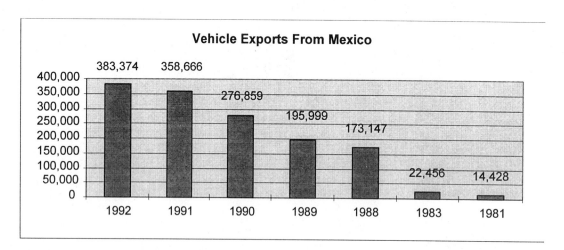

Source: Asociacion Mexicana de la Industria Automotriz (Amia)/Mexican Motor Vehicle Association

Note: Sales figures are wholesale.

EXHIBIT 2

MERCEDES BENZ - MEXICO

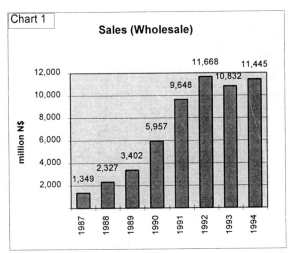

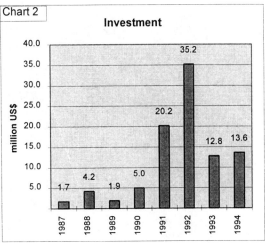

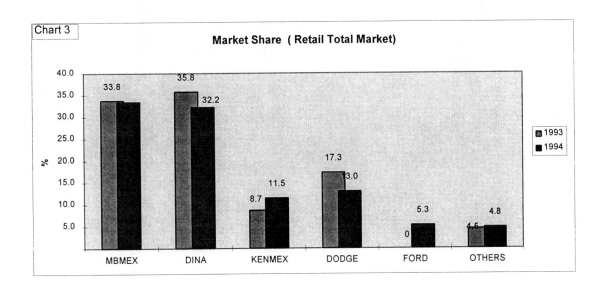

*Ford entered the market in 1994.
Source: Mercedes Benz - Mexico

EXHIBIT 3: Engine Plant, Final Assembly

EXHIBIT 4 : Truck Assembly Plant, Final Assembly

EXHIBIT 5: Car Assembly Plant, Paint Shop

Case 1.7

Ford de Mexico

Summary

Until 1994, Ford's Cuautitlan plant produced seven different car models in the same assembly line and two different truck models. The variety of models helped meet the demand for cars and trucks in the protected Mexican market. But it also caused complexity in changeover, manpower training, etc. To reduce complexity and increase productivity, Ford de Mexico now only produces variations of the Mondeo world car (the Ford Contour and Mercury Mystique) and the F-series trucks. With the devaluation of the peso and the implementation of NAFTA, it is debatable whether this policy will give Ford de Mexico a competitive advantage in the future. To maintain competitiveness in a global economy, Ford de Mexico has at least three alternatives. First, it can phase out the Mexican operations at Cuautitlan and increase imports from American plants. Second, it can become a world class competitor by upgrading equipment and producing one or two models for export. Third, it can continue with its current strategy, sit out the recession, and await further market developments.

Current Economic Situation in Mexico

On December 20, 1994, the finance minister Serra Puche announced the amplification of the exchange rate band by 13%. He emphasized that this step did not signify a move to devalue the peso but rather a measure to defend international reserves. However, the market panicked and a capital flight of $3.5 billion ensued. The exchange rate closed at 3.45N$: US$1 on that day. That night the Central Bank of Mexico announced the free floating of the new peso versus the dollar. The next day the parity opened at 5.60N$: US$1. On March 23, 1995, the exchange rate soared to 7.20N$: US$1, although it slipped slightly to 6.20N$: US$1 the next day.

After the peso devaluation, Mexico experienced a number of setbacks. Three months after President Zedillo took office (on December 1, 1994), the national stock exchange index had plummeted more than 1000 points. Interest rates reached all time highs. The average interbank rate (TIP) in March, 1995 was 109%.

The Mexican government took a variety of actions to mitigate effects of the devaluation. A monetary policy for stimulating the export sector was put in place. The first two months of 1995 showed favorable foreign trade performance: the deficit was only US$78 million compared to US$3 billion the year before. In February 1995, Mexico experienced a trade surplus of US$452 million.

On March 9, 1995, the Mexican government announced an economic program comprised of various drastic measures. The value added tax increased from 10% to 15% and the prices for electricity and gasoline increased immediately by 20% and 35%, respectively. The public sector slashed expenditure by almost

This case was written by Will Austin, Himawan Handoyo and Carol Miu-Ling Ng, MBA students in 1995 in the Max M. Fisher College of Business, The Ohio State University, under the supervision of Professors Roberto Garcia, Stephen Hills, and G. Keong Leong. This case was written for class discussion and does not necessarily imply good or poor management practices.

10%. In April 1995, the minimum salary increased 10% despite a reduction in real wages. The banking system was backed with $3 billion credit by international institutions and a restructuring of debt was planned.

In 1994, several other factors needed to be considered in evaluating the Mexican economy. The official government projections for 1995 forecast a 2% decrease in the GDP, inflation of 42%, and a current account deficit of $2 billion. The exchange rate was predicted to be 6N$: US$1 throughout 1995.

Automotive Industry in Mexico Before NAFTA[1]

As of 1995, Mexico's automotive industry was still highly regulated despite changes made through NAFTA. From September 1, 1962 imports of autos and trucks had been restricted. Regulations were contained in *The Decree for the Development and Modernization of the Automotive Industry*, first published on December 11, 1989, and consisting of two decrees. First, the automotive decree regulated passenger cars and light and medium trucks and stipulated rules governing the relationships between the light vehicle assemblers and their suppliers. Second, the autotransport decree applied to heavy trucks, truck tractors, and buses.

The Automotive Decree. (light vehicles) This decree not only liberalized the industry but also provided continued protection to existing assemblers as well as the domestic auto parts sectors. Some important liberalizations were:

1) For the first time, passenger cars and trucks could be imported,

2) No restrictions existed on the number of models each manufacturer could produce,

3) The assembler had the prerogative rights to choose either domestic or foreign suppliers, and

4) Foreigners could obtain majority ownership in auto parts companies, instead of the previously imposed 40%.

Restrictions as of 1989 were the following:

1) Imports of passenger cars and light trucks, such as minivans and sport-utility vehicles, could not exceed 15% of Mexican vehicle sales (in unit terms) for the 1991 and 1992 model years, and 20% for 1993 and 1994.

2) Imports of completed vehicles had to be balanced by exports; for every peso/dollar of new imported cars the manufacturer had to export 2.5 pesos/dollars for the 1991 model year, 2.0 for each of the 1992 and 1993 model years, and 1.75 for the 1994 model year.

3) Positive trade balances were required if assemblers were to qualify for imports.

4) At least 36% of the value of the components of vehicles sold in the domestic market had to be sourced from the local Mexican supplier industry.

---

[1] Marc Scheinmann, *Mexico's Motor Vehicle Industry: Prospects to 2000,"* The Economist Intelligence Unit, 1991, pp. 89-96.
Marc Scheinmann, *Mexico Automotive Outlook: Taking Off with NAFTA,"* Ward's Communication, 1993, pp. 17-21.

5)   A restriction on the import of subcompact cars (those with 1800cc engines or less) was valid only until the 1993 model year.

The Autotransport Decree. (trucks, tractors, and buses) This decree limited the number of autotransport units imported into Mexico if (1) the value of the imports did not exceed the value produced by the assemblers in Mexico, and (2) the foreign budget requirement --1 peso/dollar of imports to be matched with an equal value of exports -- was not violated.

Secondly, limits on value added requirements were to be lifted gradually. Up until certain dates -- January 1, 1991 for buses, January 1, 1993 for truck tractors, and January 1, 1994 for heavy trucks -- at least 40% of the national value-added sources had to come from the domestic supplier industry. After these dates, no value added requirements would exist.

The Automotive Industry in Mexico Immediately Before and After NAFTA[2]

By international standards the output of the Mexican automotive industry has always been small. For example, in 1990 (see Exhibit 1), when production and sales achieved new records, only about 820,000 vehicles were sold, and of these only about 541,000 were for the domestic market. Size has prevented the assemblers from achieving the economies of scale that enable them to produce cars and trucks efficiently and offer their vehicles at competitive international prices.

In addition, the assemblers' efficiency has been hurt by two factors. First, a greater diversity of models is frequently produced in Mexican plants than is produced abroad. For example, while it is normal to limit production to two models per plant in Japan and the USA, in Mexico the number is sometimes as high as six. Second, the continued existence of the non-tariff barriers have prevented vehicle manufacturers from integrating their Mexican operations into their global production plans. That is, performance requirements for exports, local content requirements, import restrictions, and foreign investment laws prohibit non-Mexican companies from holding a majority interest in auto parts businesses.

Limits on imports (restricted to 15% of domestic passenger car sales in 1991), export performance requirements, and limitations on ownership have raised the cost of producing vehicles in Mexico. Despite these obstacles, the industry has experienced rapid growth in hopes of greater liberalization down the line. This will allow assemblers to obtain economies of scale and develop manufacturing capabilities needed to produce world class quality automobiles.

Until a few years ago, exports were so minimal and government regulations so restrictive that the only market to consider was the domestic one. Of 597,118 vehicles produced in Mexico in 1981, 582,690 were produced for the domestic market. From 1988 to 1990, when the government began to liberalize the non-tariff barrier, the growth rate of export production was 59.5%, nearly the same rate as the domestic production growth rate of 60.3%.

It was clear to the Mexican and US participants in the NAFTA negotiations that further growth of the market in Mexico, especially the export market, could not occur unless more non-tariff barriers (NTBs) were eliminated. The transition period for NAFTA is 10 years for passenger cars and light trucks and five

---

[2]   Marc Scheinmann, *Mexico's Motor Vehicle Industry: Prospects to 2000,"* The Economist Intelligence Unit, 1991, pp. 89-96.
        Marc Scheinmann, *Mexico Automotive Outlook: Taking Off with NAFTA,"* Ward's Communication, 1993, pp. 17-21.

years for autotransport (buses, heavy trucks and truck tractors). Apart from tariff liberalization, three formidable types of NTBs will gradually be eliminated under NAFTA:

- Trade-balancing requirements (compensation for imports) to avoid large trade deficits,

- Minimum Mexican-content rules that ensure locally owned suppliers will participate in industry growth, and

- Limitations on foreign investment in the Mexican auto-parts industry aimed at preventing vertical integration.

The tariff liberalization measures and the systematic dismantling of Mexico's NTB suggest that there will be tremendous bilateral trade and investment surges over NAFTA's 10-year transition period. Mexico will certainly become the target of more American vehicle exports. It will also attract large amounts of foreign investment from industry newcomers as well as companies already established in Mexico.

As of January 1, 1994, the Mexican government removed both the unit quota on vehicle imports that was pegged to domestic sales and the trade balancing requirements for cars and trucks in dollar terms. Two new trade-balancing rules for vehicle producers were established under NAFTA. First, passenger car and light truck imports were to be balanced against exports at a 1:1 ratio. Secondly, from January 1, 1994 to December 31, 1998, autotransport companies were to be allowed to import at least 50% of the vehicles they produced in Mexico.

Before NAFTA was implemented, the Mexican government required manufacturers of cars and light trucks in Mexico to meet certain percentages of local content. Since the quality performance of the local suppliers was below average, the cost of quality control was substantial. This quality cost would offset the cost benefit vehicle manufacturers realized from cheap labor. However, under NAFTA, all local-content requirements (VANt) for passenger cars will be systematically eliminated by January 1, 2004. This will enable assemblers to reduce their production cost significantly because of savings from quality control cost for imported parts. During the transition period, the Mexican government imposed the following percentages of national value-added content: 34% for 1994-1998; 33% for 1999; 32% for 2000; 31% for 2001; 30% for 2002; and 29% for 2003. For suppliers outside the NAFTA region, the old content requirements of 36% would still hold.

The government granted an exception for Chrysler, Ford, General Motors, Nissan, and Volkswagen because they were in Mexico prior to model year 1992. These automakers could substitute their actual 1992 VANt percentage for the ones required in the 10-year transition schedule as long as 1992's ratio was lower than the one in the schedule. No changes were made for autotransport's VANt requirement since under the Autotransport Decree, VANt requirements were to be lifted as of January 1, 1994 anyway.

Ford's major competitors in Mexico are: Chrysler, General Motors, Nissan, and Volkswagon. Exhibit 2 shows the location, target market, and market share of the five major vehicle producers in Mexico; Exhibit 3 shows their assembly plant capacity.

Chrysler. Chrysler has participated in the Mexican market since the birth of the motor industry. Its current installed capacity of 190,000 to 200,000 vehicles has not changed appreciably since the mid 1980s, but the company will have to add capacity to build another 100,000 to 125,000 by 1996. In addition, the company plans to move production from its Mexico City truck plant to a new plant in Saltillo for the '95 model year. The company has high hopes for the Neon, which replaced the Shadow in Mexico's most

General Motors. With facilities equipped to manufacture 170,000 to 175,000 cars and trucks, GM has the smallest installed capacity of Mexico's five major vehicle producers. However, unlike the other manufacturers, the company has focused on truck rather than auto sales. Responding to this capacity shortage and the expectation of strong domestic sales increase, GM plans to replace its Mexico City truck plant with an expanded facility in Silao in the state of Guanajuato. GM is also revising its Car Production Program, which has been built largely around its Cavalier. It will start production of its Opel Corsa small car to compete with the Escort, Neon, Nissan Tsuru, and Golf.

Nissan. Nissan first arrived Mexico in the early 1970s but quickly established itself as a niche manufacturer of small, relatively inexpensive vehicles. The Tsuru has been sensationally successful in the Mexican market (19.8% market share in 1993), but is experiencing increasingly fierce competition from the new Ford, Chrysler, and GM entries, as well as from its traditional rival, Volkswagon. In 1993 Nissan introduced the Tsubame station wagon, a variant of a Sentra model offered in Japan, and began to increase its exports, especially to Central and South America.

Volkswagen. Volkswagen started production in Mexico in 1964. Its installed capacity of 250,000 has been increased to 300,000 in 1994, double its 1987-1988 output. In 1994, two-thirds of this output was devoted to Jettas and Golfs and only one-third to the classic Beetles that remain favorites among taxi drivers. Volkswagen's Passat and Audi models are serious contenders for entering the Mexican luxury car market. In addition, the company will become a powerful exporter, particularly to the US and Canada, since its exports already account for 70% of all Volkswagen vehicles sold.

New Entrants. Mercedes started assembly of E-class and C-class cars in Mexico in 1993 from semi-knocked-down units imported from Germany. Honda and BMW will begin production in late 1995. Other auto makers like Volvo, Toyota, Mitsubishi, and Mazda are also considering production in Mexico.

Ford de Mexico

Ford established a national company in Mexico in 1925 and began assembling cars a year later in a rented warehouse in Mexico City. Foundry operations, engine manufacturing and car/truck assembly are at Cuautitlan, a Mexico City suburb. Engine manufacturing is in Chihuahua which began operations in 1983 and is devoted to export.

While the Cuautitlan plant is comparatively old, the new plant in Hermosillo (1986) has state-of-the-art technology and a production capacity of 170,000 vehicles per year. It is fully equipped with industrial robots and a work team trained in Japan by Mazda, Ford's alliance partner. This plant builds the Mercury Tracer and the Ford Escort. Nearly all production of both car lines is exported to the United States and Canada.

Ford de Mexico is an important part of Ford's multinational operations. Its sales represented 1.52% of Ford's world wide sales in 1993, and will likely become more important with time. In April 1994, Alex Trotman, Chairman and Chief Executive Officer, announced that Ford would realign its worldwide automotive business during the next few years to move to a single set of global processes and systems in product development, manufacturing, distribution, and sales.

With the merger of the company's European and North American Automotive Operations on January 1, 1995, all automotive businesses around the world were consolidated into a new organization named Ford Automotive Operations (FAO). Five vehicle centers will be created and given global responsibility for the design, development, and engineering of new vehicles. Ford's new Global Car Program - the European Mondeo (introduced in 1993) and the North American-built Ford Contour and Mercury

Mystique (introduced in 1994) - represents a first step in combining international capabilities in the design and development of vehicles. These cars will be sold in 73 markets worldwide.

Cuautitlan Plant

The Cuautitlan site is characterized by three factories, a large warehouse of 235,000 square feet, a railroad, and a water treatment plant.

Since 1994, plant management reported directly to the U.S. headquarters. This is part of Ford's regional sales and production strategy post-NAFTA, whereby North America is treated as one huge sales market. However, no significant plant organization changes were necessary because they were already replicating a typical American plant structure.

Ford has an empowerment program which allows managers to operate with greater latitude in Mexico than in other emerging market countries. Each facility consists of a site manager, support managers, and area managers.

Ford originally established this plant to meet local demand, building seven different models in the same line. Ghia, Tempo, Topaz, Taurus, Cougar, Thunderbird, and Grand Marquis cars were manufactured, as well as two pickups classified as commercial vehicles, the F-150 and F-250. It also produced chassis for the F-350, and a P-350 chassis RS that is used for its microbus platform. This large number of models caused complexity in processing, changeover, and training, and resulted in lower productivity and less efficiency.

On January 1, 1994, the Mexican government removed the unit quota on import vehicles. Ford therefore had the option of importing vehicles to meet the domestic demand instead of producing everything locally. As of 1995, the plant produced only the F-series trucks, Contour, and Mystique (Contour and Mystique were also produced in the Kansas City plant). The reduction in the number of models decreased complexity and increased productivity. This reduction also aligned Ford de Mexico with Ford's regional and worldwide production strategy.

To increase the production capacity of Contour and Mystique to 108,000 annually, the Cuautitlan plant was expanded and upgraded in 1994 with a $60 million reported investment, mainly in tools and equipment (actual expenditure was about $100 million). The planned 1995 output, headcount and parts count are shown in Exhibit 4. Exhibit 5 shows the sales composition by product type and market from 1988 to 1993.

Peso Devaluation

The economic crisis of 1995 caught Ford's management somewhat by surprise because economically, Mexico's situation appeared fundamentally sound for an emerging market. Political issues triggered the devaluation and Ford's management was reminded of how important politics are to the country's economy. After the devaluation, Ford estimated (in a worst case scenario) that sales would drop by 50% and inflation and interest rates would increase. As of 1995, Ford operated on a self-standing basis financially. All funds were generated through sales and domestic borrowing, and futures were utilized to hedge against exchange rate fluctuation.

In response to its new environment, Ford made adjustments in human resources, marketing, operations, and supply. These adjustments dealt with the short-run problem of peso devaluation and the long-run problems associated with Ford's regional and worldwide sales/production strategies.

Human Resources

A key issue facing Ford is how to maintain employee morale in an increasingly volatile market environment. In the past, Ford had increased wages according to the guidelines suggested by the government. Ford assisted its employees through meal subsidies, transportation assistance, and food coupons, etc. Traditionally, Ford laid off people during economic downturns without explanation or advance warning. They preferred the short-term option of cutting costs through layoffs rather than the long-term option of retaining workers and investing in them (i.e., training the workforce during economic downturns).

Currently, Ford uses a different, more open approach with its employees. They discuss issues facing the company with the workers and provide advance notice of operational changes. Time is taken to ensure that employees understand the personnel decisions of top management. With the current economic crisis, Ford has used staggered work schedules (i.e., work one week, rest the next week) and voluntary vacations to maintain employees and offset excess capacity. In addition, the company works closely with its unions. Worldwide competition helps create common interest between the company and its unions.

Marketing

The peso devaluation affects domestic and foreign market demands differently. In the domestic market, devaluation raises the costs of imported parts in Mexican produced cars. If car prices remain the same, profits will go down as production costs increase. In the export market, devaluation will lower the export price of the car and increase sales if demand is elastic, which it should be for small cars. Luxury cars produced in Mexico are unaffected domestically or internationally because they are relatively price inelastic in demand. The most important effect of devaluation is the accompanying rise in interest rates which immediately depresses domestic demand for small cars since most people must finance their purchase.

After the devaluation, Ford's management felt there was little marketing could do to positively influence consumer buying behavior. Incentives for sales and marketing would be ineffective, and demand for automotive financing services very low due to 100% nominal interest rates. Therefore, marketing decided to focus on the positive aspects of the country and people. For example, Ford sponsored the South American Folkloric Art Exhibition, in order to maintain a positive image while sales demand was low.

Because of high inventory levels before the crisis, Ford faced the loss of many of its dealers. Maintaining high inventory is especially costly during inflationary devaluation. Ford stripped down its models and lowered prices to make sales more attractive. But because of high inventory levels, Ford and the dealers were forced to lower prices even more. To end this downward pricing spiral, Ford extended non-monetary incentives and equipment to the dealers, which are more difficult for the competition to match.

Operations/ Supply Issues

Ford requires all Mexican suppliers to use Just-in-Time (JIT) delivery methods. Approximately 70% of suppliers are located very close to the Cuautitlan plant (within 1/2 hour's drive). The number of suppliers is much lower than in the US (there are only 80 national suppliers to Cuautitlan). This makes managing JIT at the local level a little easier. However, parts imported from the US, Canada, and Europe have 15-16 day transit times, and are consequently kept at higher inventory levels.

Because of NAFTA's new rules, the local supplier network is not as important an issue for Ford as it is to Volkswagen. Whereas Ford can import from US suppliers, Volkswagen needs its suppliers in Mexico to comply with content rules (they do not have operations in Canada or the U.S. to help them). Therefore, Volkswagen is more dependent on local suppliers than its competitors.

Currently, Ford de Mexico produces with 40% Mexican value-added (measured in terms of dollars) including those units that are exported to North America. In selecting local suppliers, Ford focuses on quality, location, and price. Even though the local content requirement will be eliminated by January 1, 2004, Ford is planning to keep relationships with its Mexican suppliers as long as these suppliers maintain their competitiveness in quality, delivery, and price.

Conclusion

Ford de Mexico must make both short and long term decisions to assure future success, and it must make the decisions in the face of considerable uncertainty. In the short run, it must adjust to a devaluation-induced recession. Its long run decisions need to complement short run strategy.

In order to maintain competitiveness in the long run, Ford de Mexico can choose from at least three alternatives for its Cuautitlan plant. First, it can phase out inefficient production, close its plant at Cuautitlan, and increase imports from high volume American plants. Second, it can install state-of-the-art technology and make the Cuautitlan plant a world class manufacturer of sub-compact cars. Third, it can continue with the existing strategy, try to increase the export of small cars in the US, wait for short-term currency problems to pass, and await further developments.

Questions for students

1. What are some of the human resource implications of adopting one or another of the three possible long run strategies?

2. How could Ford de Mexico make each of the three long run strategies compatible with the short run requirements of adjusting to the recession?

3. What are the pros and cons of adopting each of the strategies?

4. Which one would you adopt and why?

Exhibit 1:   **Mexican Vehicle Production and Sales (1981-1992)**

Year	Production	Total Sales	Domestic	Exports
1992	1,083,091	1,090,288	706,914	383,374
1991	989,373	992,276	633,610	358,666
1990	820,576	821,798	544,939	276,859
1989	641,281	641,863	445,864	195,999
1988	512,776	515,066	341,919	173,147
1983	285,485	295,271	272,815	22,456
1981	597,118	585,441	571,013	14,428

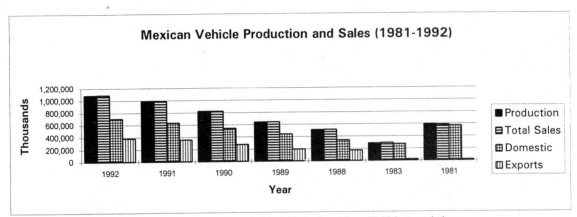

Source: Asociacion Mexicana de la Industria Automotriz (Amia)/ Mexican Motor Vehicle Association
Note: Sales figures are wholesale

Exhibit 2:   **Mexico Assembly Plant Capacities (units)**

Assembly Plant	Straight-Time Capacity	Cars	Trucks	1992 Actual Output
Ford	290,000	170,000	120,000	257,000
Chrysler	200,000	125,000	75,000	235,000
GM	175,000	105,000	70,000	200,000
Nissan	200,000	150,000	50,000	173,000
VW	250,000	235,000	15,000	189,000
Total	1,115,000	785,000	330,000	1,054,000

Exhibit 3: Planned 1995 Output, Headcount and Parts Count

Car Assembly (units)

Contour	51,013
Mystique E	18,157
Mystique L	9,178
Grand Marquis (Phase Out)	4,697
Total	**83,045**

Truck Assembly (units)

F-150	6,402
F-250	7,958
F-350	11,008
Total	**25,368**

Workers (people)

	Hourly	Salary
Assembly	3,300	400
Foundry	255	48
Engines	398	56

Parts Counts (units)

Contour/Mystique	2,814
F-Series	1,229
Grand Marquis	1,043
Total	**5,086**

Exhibit 4: Ford Sales Composition by Product Type and Market
1988 - 1993 (%)

Year	Domestic		Export	
	Cars	Trucks	Cars	Trucks
1993	28.8	18.9	52.4	0
1992	26.3	22.8	50.9	0
1991	25.1	25.2	49.7	0
1988	25	23.2	51.8	0

Case 1.8

BEIJING BRICK FACTORY

Summary

A Chinese factory that employs about 800 people in making bricks is given the responsibility of pricing and selling its own products to a variety of customers (and not just to another government agency as was true under the previous system of central planning.) The brick factory faces two serious problems. It is in search of a joint venture partner to provide capital for upgrading its technology. And its principle supply of clay is running out due to the exhaustion of supplies on the land leased by the firm.

You are associated with the Center for Technology Transfer of a major U.S. university and have been contacted by the representative of a firm in China dedicated to finding joint venture partners for Chinese firms. The Center identifies companies that may be interested in international business ventures and assists them in finding partnerships in other countries. You have visited a firm located outside Beijing and have been asked to write up a report containing information on two future business strategies that you think might make good economic sense. The report will be given to a U.S. firm interested in a Chinese partnership. For each business strategy, you should spell out the possibilities you see for increasing profits (you can suggest new lines of work, new ways of organizing the current work, etc.) Secondly, you should identify what the human resource implications are for each strategy you choose. Identify the people whose lives would be improved and the people whose lives would be harmed by each strategy. Note any special factors you must you take into account due to China's unique history.

The Factory

About 800 people are employed at the factory. All live in company housing. The factory produces bricks. The earth for the bricks is obtained from an open pit at the rear of the company's land. The pit has grown bigger over the years and encompasses most of the land area right up to the boundary of the company's property. Surrounding the company are small plots of land used for farming by families whose community once owned all the property in the area communally. Since the reforms of Deng Xiao Ping, the brick factory has leased its land from the community in which it is located. Farms nearby are also leased to families that work the land. Within several years, the brick factory's supply of clay from the pit will have been exhausted.

Bricks are formed from the clay and placed in kilns to bake. Outdated machinery is used to produce the bricks. Small Chinese-made tractors are used to haul the bricks from place to place, but much hand labor is required to stack the bricks in the kilns and to move them on and off the carts. Coal is used to fire the kilns and is brought into the factory by truck. Fairly large inventories of coal must be kept on hand to provide energy since suppliers are not reliable and often the factory must rely on its inventories while waiting for new truckloads to arrive. The increase in the income of farmers that has come about due to

This case was prepared by Professors Stephen Hills, The Ohio State University, and Keyong Dong, People's University, China, for class discussion and does not necessarily imply either good or poor management practices.

Deng's reforms has resulted in steady demand for bricks to use in the construction of houses for farmers. The houses are constructed in the ancient Chinese style of a small compound for each family, walled in by bricks, with a central courtyard and houses opening out onto the courtyard on three sides. For new hotels and office buildings in the larger cities, bricks are being replaced by other building materials.

In the past, workers have been assigned to the factory from a centralized employment bureau in Beijing. However, the factory manager is now finding that people assigned to it do not want to come out from Beijing to work. Thus, workers must come from the agricultural community nearby. Even at that, new workers are hard to find since the work is very difficult. Wages are low, but overstaffing of the factory means that people do not have to work a full day.

Jobs were once life-long, but the system is changing. Most young workers are now employed on five-year contracts. Employers are able to hire workers at job fairs in the region. During times of slack work, an employer is more apt to cut wages than to directly lay-off workers.

Workers are able to afford some stereo equipment, a TV, and a small refrigerator. Kitchens and bathrooms are communal in the apartment block housing. What families want most at the present time are telephones. About half of the workers have phones that are owned and operated by the factory through its own switchboard. The factory provides medical care for employees. When a worker retires, he or she continues to live in company housing.

Bicycles are the main form of transportation. It takes about 30 minutes to ride by bicycle from the factory to the outskirts (Summer Palace) of Beijing. Bus transportation is also possible along the main road into the city. The Summer Palace, a beautiful park built for recreation of the (once) Emperor's family, lies on the outskirts of Beijing, in the direction of the brick factory. The park is now a major tourist attraction in Beijing.

Profit margins for the brick factory are modest, about four percent on sales. At one time, all profits from the factory were claimed by local government authorities and bricks were produced according to directives by the local government. The local plan was a part of the larger national plan, containing national goals for construction materials. Now the firm is allowed to keep its profits with a certain amount being paid to the government in taxes. But it now must also find buyers for the bricks. A certain amount of its production is guaranteed for government purchase with the rest sold to whomever wants to buy.

The general manager of the factory was previously the chairman of the communist party's political committee in the factory. In his previous position he had considerable influence over the policies of the firm. But his successor has less influence since Deng's reforms. Now authority for the operation of the factory has shifted greatly to the general manager. He replaced the former general manager who has now moved over to occupy the position of president of the factory's own labor union. Traditionally, when a general manager nears the age of retirement, he is appointed to be president of the company's labor union.

Questions for students

1.   Write your report and suggest two strategies that could be used by the firm to solve its problems

2.   What are the human resource implications of each strategy?

3.   Would the strategies you select be different in the Chinese firm than if the firm were located in the U.S.? Why or why not?

Case 1.9

FROM RUSSIA WITH LOVE

Summary

The end of the Cold War opened many opportunities for exchange between Russia and the West, particularly in the areas of manufacturing, distribution, and service systems. Russia's movement toward a Western-style market economy may have a greater impact in areas like Ekaterinburg (during the Soviet period, Sverdlovsk), a formerly closed city and center of heavy and defense industries in Western Siberia. This case describes current manufacturing conditions in Ekaterinburg and requires a business decision briefing to assess future directions for this corporate endeavor.

Bill Stone sank slowly into his stuffed office chair and gazed absently out the corner window into the gray winter city scape of Chicago. It had been a tough day and he was still tired from his recent trip to Ekaterinburg. The eleven hour time difference, the extreme cold of Siberia, and the never-ending rounds of social activities offered by his Russian hosts had taken their toll. Yet the Joint Agreement between the American Mining Equipment Company and the Urals Machine Consortium had tremendous promise, despite the problems. Both companies were major international manufacturers of mining and excavating equipment, such as steam shovels and ore trucks. As the recently appointed Director of Operations of AME, it was his job to make the Joint Agreement work.

Bill routinely thumbed through the day's mail. then turned to his computer, where the icon in the corner announced the receipt of a new e-mail message.

> Dear Bill; (it read)
>
> Hope return travel to Chicago was good and not too tired, and you have now time to discuss our meetings and situation with joint agreement.
>
> We so pleased your visit to us and thanks for all assistants. Much we have done since you leave. Heavy shovel assembly committee did meet and discuss plans for revised schedule and Director was discussed with Region Planning Committee needs for more space in manufacturing and problems of chimney gasses.
>
> We thank to you for wonderful friendship; Galena sends best greetings to Eva Maria.
>
> Most sincerely
>
> Nicholai Antonovich

This case was prepared by Professors Peter W. Stonebraker, Northeastern Illinois University and Sergey Nicholaevivh Polbitsyn, Urals State Pedagogic University, for class discussion and does not necessarily imply either good or poor management practices. The authors would like to express their appreciation for support in this project from the U.S. Information Service, the Soros Foundation, Northeastern Illinois University, Urals State Pedagogic University, and Urals State Vocational Pedagogical University.

Bill's thoughts wandered slowly through the cold mists of Chicago to Ekaterinburg, almost half a world away. Ekaterinburg was located in the Ural mountains (Americans would call it Siberia), but definitely on the Western edge, or gateway, to the extensive Siberian resources. In Soviet times, Ekaterinburg was called Sverdlovsk; now it was the third largest city in the Russian Federation, after Moscow, the national capital, and Saint Petersburg, on the Baltic. For many years during the Cold War, Ekaterinburg was closed due to the military and defense industries there. Foreigners could not enter the city and residents were not permitted to leave without prior authorization. Gary Powers, the American U-2 spy pilot, had been shot down there and, even today, many plants are known only by numbers which were assigned to conceal their identity and the nature of their production.

However, Nicholai Antonovich and Galena Ivanovna, his wife, had been such wonderful hosts. The five-day visit had been full of activities. There were trips to the opera and symphony, both among the best in Russia, visits to family homes where Bill was given the position of honor sitting on the sofa at the family dinner table and entertained with piano and violin recitals by family members and slide presentations of family camping trips to the Black Sea.

But the days had been all business. Breakfasts of strong instant coffee, rolls and cheese and sausage, hosted by the Director General of UMC, Vladimir Fyodorov, and attended by Deputy Directors and staff members, started with polite inquiries about family and accommodations. But conversation quickly focused toward specific topics, defined by the Joint Agreement, such as the product mix or the schedule of technology transfers. Bill had been advised by AME staff and colleagues that there was extensive interest in UMC, particularly from former Soviet Block and Eastern European nations. Dinner, in the middle of the day, was more formal; silver chafing dishes and four or five courses, starting with soup and bread, then salad, an entree with vegetables and potatoes, and a dessert.

Mornings and afternoons involved plant tours, meetings with staff and committee groups, government officials and private bankers. At one such meeting with the Governor of the Sverdlovsk Region, Bill was given strong assurances that the Joint Agreement would be supported by both regional and national governments. The Governor concluded by commenting that "Russians must learn to destroy the Iron Curtain in their minds." Bill's attempt to learn Russian had helped and was certainly appreciated by his hosts; but discussions moved slowly through Irena and Natasha, who took turns interpreting. Bill did not understand his uncomfortableness with the interpretation process; perhaps it was a matter of different interpretations or usages, perhaps it was a cultural thing, or perhaps it was just his own unfamiliarity with the process. But, though the Joint Agreement had been signed, as Bill looked deeper into the operation, he saw some inconsistencies and felt there might be further misunderstandings. John Chase, AME's President, would certainly want him to address some of these issues tomorrow at the monthly Planning Update Conference.

One very obvious question was strategic planning. The Joint Agreement was clear; AME would produce certain items of equipment for export to Russia and eastern markets and UMC would produce other items for export to America and western markets. The annual volumes and product specifications were clearly stated. This market segmentation and cooperation offered advantages to both companies, such as specialization and focus of operations, thereby reducing costs and improving efficiencies. Additionally, the integrated scheduling of their complementary, long-lead-time products would stabilize production scheduling at each company. But Bill had seen very little indication of strategic planning or long-, mid- and short- range business forecasting by his Russian counterparts, and he was concerned that Joint

Agreement deliveries from UMC might be slowed if their non-agreement business received a higher priority in the future.

His Russian colleagues had confirmed, and reconfirmed, their commitment to the Joint Agreement; and they had apologized for the extreme turbulence of the government regulatory environment, the financial environment, and their lack of solid planning and forecasting data. In fact, they described for Bill some examples of vacillating taxation, environmental, and safety policies.

Two years ago, for example, a 100% tax increase, based on product value, had been levied on all facilities that generated sulphur emissions, even very low levels. Products within the Joint Agreement were exempted because taxes on exports were stable, but other UMC production was not. It took six months of lobbying and numerous defaults and bankruptcies to convince the government to change the tax. Then, one day, a letter was forwarded from the Central Economic Committee to the Regional Economic Committee and then to affected companies that the tax had been canceled and the Minister for Environmental Affairs had been fired.

Several conversations with Derwin Karsten, the Shop Master at Factory 14 and UMC employee for 52 years, were also difficult to ignore. Derwin had described for Bill the movement of the plant from Leningrad (now St. Petersburg) in 1941, just before the Nazi Army blockaded the city where he lived, and he commented on his many years as production manager under the Soviet central planning system. Derwin's job, it seemed to Bill, had been to implement a plan, which was often politically inspired. Derwin described rail cars with Bills of Transportation showing equipment contents that, in fact, were shipped empty and commissioners who minimized their contributions to production so they could be sure to make their personal quotas. Yet, when asked about the future of Russian manufacturing, Derwin commented with a grin:

> "Now that... the future, it be fun. But we have many work to do, so we get rapidly started. But, problem is ... worker know how to work, but manager understand only how to work under ... strict plans."

> "When plant was evacuated from Leningrad and started to issue military goods here, military officers appeared on plant floor with duty to check quantity and quality of issued production ... and report to Moscow. If person produced bad good, he could even be named as 'sabotaznick' and disappear in Gulag."

> "But also, if you make any suggestion on improving production, you could be granted with additional food and even free day for rest. Later all these stimulations disappeared. Nobody invented anything new and (a touch of bitterness marked Derwin's voice) we lost our growth skills and no longer worked properly to educate worker in technical matters."

> "But," Derwin grinned, "Russian worker with help of friends and comrades do anything. Russian worker know how to be teams and to work for good of all."

There were other problems. Orders were canceled because of the lack of state or private funding. The ruble had inflated by 50% in the past year, and by 600% in the prior year. During that turbulence, however, the dollar price of goods varied by less than 20% per year. Bill had to concede that the several forecasts he had seen, with annual errors of greater than 70%, had been done correctly, and that in such conditions, strategic planning and forecasting were tough. But he continued to be concerned with what appeared to be a general disregard for careful planning, forecasting, and scheduling.

Bill again reviewed several translations of the long range forecasts provided by UMC (Table 1) . Valerie Larionov, Chief of the Economic Planning Department, had provided the quarterly and annual planning data, with the base line simple moving average (sma) and initial Winter's method ($\alpha = .2$, $\beta = .1$, $\Gamma = .1$) forecasts. Mechanically, the data appeared to be correct, but the high error rates bothered Bill. He wondered if lagging or aggregating the data might improve the results. Forecasting with small unit values is always difficult.

Table 1

Strategic Forecasts for Heavy Mining Equipment
Russian Federation Market
(new customer orders per period)

Year	Quarter	RUS 6 Actual (projected)	Forcast (2sma)	Forecast (Winter's)	RUS 8 Actual (Projected)	Forcast (2sma)	Forecast (Winter's)
1	I	4		3.68	2		3.07
	II	6		4.47	1		1.59
	III	5	5	5.96	5	1.5	2.11
	IV	8	5.5	10.41	3	3	4.19
2	I	2	6.5	4.73	7	4	4.22
	II	6	5	5.04	2	5	2.55
	III	5	4	6.18	1	4.5	3.86
	IV	10	5.5	10.48	3	1.5	4.65
3	I	7	7.5	4.68	3	2	4.84
	II	2	8.5	6.52	4	3	2.23
	III	9	4.5	6.46	2	3.5	3.77
	IV	16	5.5	12.25	9	3	4.93
4(plan)	I	8	12.5	6.03	5	5.5	6.25
	II	8			5		
	III	9			5		
	IV	9			5		
5(plan)	I	9			6		
	II	9			6		
	III	10			6		
	IV	10			6		
6(plan)	(annual)	40			25		
7(plan)	(annual)	44			28		

The facilities visits had also been very interesting. Ivan Okhrimenko, Chief Deputy Engineer, had spent several days explaining the production flows and capital equipment. Most of the production equipment was older; a few lathes were American, dating from the Lend-Lease Program in the 1930s. Plant equipment, though generally older in design, was clean and well- maintained. Numerous replacement and spare parts had been designed and manufactured locally. Some European computer-controlled equipment supplemented the generalized equipment, and workers appeared skilled with either technology, but, on several occasions, expressed a need for state-of-the-art computer-assisted-manufacturing equipment. In fact, Bill saw little indication of automation during his entire visit. Bar codes were not used, either by UMC or in the retail stores, and such activities as scheduling, inventory management, and forecasting were all done manually, or by a recently-trained university economics professor.

Some materials, particularly case hardened steel, were held in excess of expected needs, while other materials, usually rubber and plastic parts, were expedited on a weekly basis. Shortages in numerous commodities had resulted in the development of a secondary dealer-to-dealer market. Maintenance, though very carefully managed, was done only when equipment broke down.

Quality control appeared to be the responsibility of the workers, not management, but the equipment designs tolerated variances in manufacturing specifications. Engines required a surprisingly long run-in time of 20 hours, and Ivan explained that "if it will run for 20 hours, it's OK". Bill had also attended several training sessions in statistical process control given by a university professor, and had reviewed several initial quality analyses (Table 2).

Table 2

Statistical Process Control Data for Engine Valves
(radius in millimeters)
BMC 12 and BMC 16

| | BMC 12 Observation | | | | | | BMC 16 Observation | | | | |
Lot #	1	2	3	4	5	Lot #	1	2	3	4	5
1	46.3	48.1	47.7	46.5	47.2	1	22.3	21.7	23.1	12.2	22.3
2	47.7	45.9	47.6	46.3	46.4	2	23.5	21.3	20.4	22.6	22.5
3	47.6	47.8	48.1	47.6	46.3	3	22.8	26.2	20.8	21.6	22.6
4	46.9	47.7	46.2	47.4	47.4	4	23.2	23.7	22.5	22.9	16.9
5	47.8	48.1	46.4	45.9	47.7	5	22.6	21.9	20.4	22.8	23.1

The production process appeared to be labor intense. In fact, Ivan stated that it was very costly to fire workers because the company would have to contribute six months' salary to the worker's unemployment compensation. Thus, many companies, including UMC, had resorted to under paying workers or skipping monthly pay checks. Even so, UMC was supportive of its labor force, which averaged nineteen years of employment with the company. Bill had spoken with several workers who were owed several months of back-pay; but who proudly carried ownership stock of the company which had been paid, instead of cash. Though many executives openly expressed a need for improved technology and training, most also noted that implementation of new technologies would not result in reductions of the roughly 80,000 employees at the seven major production facilities in the Sverdlovsk region (roughly equivalent to a mid-sized state).

Safety appeared to be a more immediate problem. Bill noted the presence of high noise levels and no hearing protection in the engine testing room and near several of the milling operations. Additionally, most equipment did not have hand or foot safety guards. For example, Bill watched as one woman placed metal plates in a stamping machine, then with a foot trigger, released the stamp. As the machine recovered, she pulled the stamped part out with her fingers. He had asked Ivan what protected the woman's fingers; Ivan's response was to tap his finger against the side of his head and say "This". The labor force demonstrated high levels of discipline and training with the exception of some unavailable computer skills. Pay at UMC averaged about $80 per month, which (because UMC is a former state-owned business), is higher than most businesses in the area. Never-the-less, to live comfortably, family members of most employees must work. The UMC cafeteria provided free meals for employees and the company offers a relatively generous retirement plan; however, with inflation, the retirement plan was of little value.

The managers he had met impressed him. Several, who might be described as "angry young men", were in their late 30s, and had been employed by the company for some fifteen or more years. Some, like Ivan, had traveled to Western Europe to visit various companies and had developed an intuitive understanding of Western markets and industrial processes. These new managers clearly had found a common language and goal with senior laborers like Derwin and rejected the established bureaucratic directors in their organizations.

Even in his short visit, Bill had started to feel appreciation for the mystique of Russia, the vast untapped mineral and human resources, the power of life-long friendships, and the tremendous strength of stoic work ethics. As Vladimir Fyodorov had stated at the first breakfast meeting: "To do business in Russia, particularly in the Sverdlovsk area, you must become friends first."

Bill glanced at his watch, and placed the several reports back in the file folder. He considered suggesting to the Monthly Planning Update a multi-stage process to develop the Joint Agreement with UMC. But how to define the steps? What could be the impact of possible "translation misunderstandings" and "cultural differences?" Should he start with a more technical evaluation, or would a general SWOT (strengths, weaknesses, opportunities, threats) analysis be appropriate? Some of these questions would be settled when Nicholai Antonovich came to Chicago in several months, but Bill had a briefing to give tomorrow morning.

Bill tossed the folders in his briefcase and headed for the door. Eva Maria would have a good supper ready and he wanted to sleep on this one a bit.

Questions for students

1.   Do you think that Bill has enough information to go ahead with this project?   How will he know if his information is sufficient?

2.   What are the largest risks in this venture?   Are the risks more technical in nature or do they have more to do with persons who will start up the venture?

3.   What is Bill doing to minimize his risks?   What other actions would you recommend to reduce the risk?

4.   Prepare a SWOT analysis for Bill and give your recommendations about next steps based on your analysis.

SIMULATION GAME

Searching for a Joint Venture Partner

Instructions:

The class is divided into several groups. Each group is split into one team representing a potential Chinese joint venture partner (two people) and another team (can be several people) representing the American firm that is seeking a partner. Both teams review preliminary information about the proposed joint venture and general information about the partners (shown below as "The American Partner" and "The Chinese Partner").

Students representing the Chinese firm review a detailed brief on the Chinese firm's operations (below). They would like to establish a partnership with the American firm. Their task is to describe the firm's potential to the American representatives, placing themselves in as favorable a light as possible without being dishonest. Students representing the American side brainstorm among themselves to prepare key questions to ask of the Chinese. They are skeptical about whether they should establish a joint venture with the Chinese firm. Their task is to compile the information they need to decide if the joint venture can be successful. After extended discussion, both teams stop to assess whether they wish to initiate the project. The final step is for both sides to review the initial briefing given to the Chinese representatives. They identify what important areas were missed in the prior discussion and what ramifications such omissions might have had on the venture's success.

For students of international business, the simulated joint venture decision combines key issues about staffing, compensation, work force skills, and legal requirements in the context of the whole business venture's potential success. All the functional areas of business must be taken into account in the decision making process.

THE AMERICAN PARTNER

The American firm is a large company in the business of distributing various kinds of gases -- oxygen, hydrogen, etc. The firm would like to enter the same distribution market in China, but before it does so, it needs a reliable supply of storage containers for transported gases. To import the containers would be prohibitively expensive, even though the control mechanisms for the containers could be imported. The supplier should be a firm that is making similar kinds of containers. Because of the nature of the gases to be transported, the containers must be made with high quality control. The firm must have a committed work force, willing and able to learn new skills. The firm will need to control information on the new technological processes that it learns, thereby preventing adoption by competitors.

This simulation game was prepared by Professor Stephen Hills, The Ohio State University and Jia Yuan Zhao, a private business owner in Hangzhou, China.

THE CHINESE PARTNER

The firm is a village enterprise located in a small town five hours by car from Shanghai, and a half hour ferry ride across the Yangtze River. The designation "village enterprise" means that the firm is not a large, state owned firm. Rather, it is collectively owned by the small municipality in which all workers live. As a consequence, the success of the firm is important to the entire town. The firm must pay the town two million Yuan per year, but beyond that, it can retain its profits, with an annual target for profit of about six million Yuan.

The American firm discovered the Chinese firm through the Chinese firm's several very visible sales offices in the region. The firm almost went bankrupt four years ago, but now a new, young manager has been hired. Sales have doubled in each of the last three years. The firm is now profitable and meeting its targeted profit margin. It is reported that the firm has about 1,000 employees.

DETAILED BRIEF ON THE CHINESE FIRM

The Product:

The firm makes a wide variety of containers. Only 10 percent of its production consists of standardized containers. The rest are custom orders. The workforce is accustomed to learning new skills.

The Workforce:

Workers are quite young and have worked for a relatively short period of time for the firm. Most of the firm's long tenured workers quit when the firm was threatened with bankruptcy. Workers had been hired on an implied long term contract, so workers were not laid off when bankruptcy was threatened, but wages were reduced and gradually workers sought other alternatives. The new workers have also been hired on an implied long term contract. Both men and women work as welders, etc. Very little occupational segregation by sex is in evidence.

Government regulations restrict work to eight hours per day. The firm operates two twelve hour shifts per day. The general manager says that everyone wants to work so what can he do? Workers appear to be working steadily -- no one sitting without work as is more typical in the state owned enterprises. Workers use little or no protective equipment.

Only 400 of the firm's 1,000 employees actually work in the division that makes containers. Twenty of the 400 are university trained. Trained workers are hard to attract to this small town. The firm must train from within. Welders, however, all hold government certification.

Blackboards at the entrance to the firm show production levels reported by teams of workers for the prior week. Each team has its own blackboard with production for each day of the week graphed out. Key financial data for the firm are also reported on bulletin boards at the plant's entrance. ISO standards are used for quality control, but even so, the control is uneven for the containers that are being made.

The Management:

Little hierarchy appears to exist in the firm. The general manager is in his mid-30s and has good, friendly working relationships with employees. Key managerial jobs are held within the family or by a small circle of the general manager's close friends. There are no first line supervisors. Compared with state owned firms, very few managers are working in their offices but rather are circulating through the plant.

On the wall of the general manager's office are displayed the firm's organizational chart and the strategic plan for the year. To gain the technical expertise he needs, the general manger relies on outside consultants, thereby creating the possibility that innovative processes introduced to the firm might be spread to competitors.

The ownership of the firm is quite ambiguous. It is not owned exclusively by the general manager or his family, nor is it owned exclusively by the town or the employees.

Logistics:

Transportation is difficult. Roads are getting better but are crowded with all types of vehicles, and many roads are continuously under construction. Containers are transported by truck . In the next few years, a new bridge will span the Yangtze, eliminating the ferry ride.

If control mechanisms are imported, a duty free warehouse would be advantageous for importing the more advanced designs. The nearest duty free zone is relatively far away.

Finance:

Finances for the company are under the exclusive control of the general manger. No auditing is done, and the firm does not have an outside accountant.

The firm currently has enough unfilled orders to double its production. Increasing production is difficult, however, because the firm has too few overhead cranes. The firm needs capital to purchase more cranes but has used up its quota for credit from the Central Bank. Other sources of credit are hard to obtain. The firm already has plenty of land available for expansion. A new building could easily be constructed on vacant land and thereby double the firm's capacity to produce containers.

Cost plus pricing is used for the product, with a 15 percent profit margin. All orders must be paid for in full on delivery. This minimizes the possibility for long outstanding accounts receivables that would hurt cash flow.

Case 2.1

RUSSKI RESTAURANT

Summary

A petroleum distribution company in Central Russia is contemplating an investment in a micro-brewery. This investment requires an analysis of the market for imported beer in the city of Omsk, an evaluation of the equipment and capacity alternatives, and a financial analysis. A recommendation is required concerning the market segment(s) to be targeted, the micro-brewery equipment configuration, and the financial attractiveness of this investment.

Gregoriy Rasputin, Managing Director of Omsk Petroleum Company, is considering an investment proposal submitted by the Food Division of the company. This proposal concerns the installation of a micro-brewery in one of the restaurants presently owned by the company. This restaurant is located in Omsk, Siberia. If accepted, this proposal would result in the establishment of the first micro-brewery restaurant in Russia. Gregoriy's major concerns are with the profitability of this investment proposal, and the feasibility of the proposed marketing and operations strategies.

Company Background

The Omsk Petroleum Company is a recently privatized company that owns and operates both petroleum exploration and production operations in Siberia, Russia. In addition to the petroleum operations, the company owns and operates a variety of other businesses in Siberia, including several restaurants. The restaurants are located in cities where the firm has office and plant facilities, and are used primarily by company employees for lunch. In recent years the restaurant in Omsk has been run by an outside contractor. However, this arrangement has not been fully satisfactory to the company, and management has decided to take over the operation of the restaurant. The intention is to operate the restaurant at lunch time for the company's employees, and to open the restaurant in the evenings for commercial trade.

Micro Brewery Marketing Strategy

The restaurant in Omsk is an upmarket restaurant with a fantastic view of the Om river. Omsk is a city with a population of 500,000, located in the central Russian state of Siberia. The company's Marketing Director, Maria Stolychnaja, has proposed that the first floor of this restaurant be remodeled into a micro-brewery bar. The beer made in the micro-brewery could then be sold in both the bar and the restaurant.

Product Concept: The Marketing Director described the investment proposal as "an exciting new concept in the Russian restaurant and bar trade. The micro-brewing product concept represents an innovative approach designed to increase consumer awareness and interest in high quality imported beer." Maria believes that the opportunity to drink high quality German beer of the Eikorn brand in the distinctive atmosphere of an

This case was prepared by Professors William L. Berry and Martha C. Cooper of The Ohio State University and MBA students (class of 1996) Dmitry A. Shirshov (Ulyanovsk, Russia) and Elena V. Karlina (St. Petersburg, Russia). © 1996 by The Ohio State University, Columbus, Ohio 43210. This case was reprinted with permission.

authentic German beer garden would produce a major increase in the company's Omsk restaurant and bar sales volume.

Pricing: The Marketing Director has proposed a price of 12,000 Rubles for one-half liter. This is a reasonably high price in this market. An exclusive local bar sells imported Beck's beer for 11,250 per half liter.[1] Imported beer also sells in Omsk for 8,000 rubles per half liter. A check of several street kiosks in the area indicates an average price of 6,500 rubles per half liter for imported beer. In contrast, Russian-brewed beer sells for 2,300-3,000 Rubles per half-liter in the kiosks.

Promotion Plans: The Marketing Director plans to open the micro-brewery restaurant with a large public reception, and will invite leading public officials and company executives to attend this function. Advertising possibilities include word of mouth, newspaper, and some television coverage. Currently, local TV advertising consists of printed overlays during regular TV programming. National products are advertised in other TV ads. Most Omsk newspapers publish supplemental issues which contain advertisement information. The cost of an ad in such an issue varies from 220,000 Rubles to 720,000 Rubles, depending on the size of an ad. TV advertising costs are estimated to be 5,000,000 Rubles per minute.

In addition, the Marketing Director is considering a special introductory price of 8,000 rubles to last at least through the "grand opening" period. This would effect a trial of the micro-brewery concept and the beverage itself.

Market Environment

Russia is more than seven years into Perestrioka (restructuring) and movement toward a market economy. In the process, the state-owned wholesale and retail levels of distribution have basically disappeared. Many large plants in the Omsk area have been privatized. Although some of these plants have seen modest sales growth, many people have been laid off, and in some cases, the newly formed enterprises have gone out of business altogether. Unemployment is currently 7.5%. However, new businesses are springing up. Trade in all kinds of goods is occurring and ad hoc distribution systems are taking shape. Although part of the population has enjoyed higher wages and greater opportunities from the restructuring, a significant portion barely survives.

The economic conditions in terms of inflation rates and industrial production growth are not very favorable. During the last 5 years, the GNP has declined at the rate of up to 25% a year with a cumulative drop of 45%. This year was the first time the decline in production slowed and the economy showed some modest growth. Inflation has been running in the 15-25% range per month, although lately it has slowed to 4.5% (Exhibit 1). The country just received a large loan from the International Monetary Fund on condition of lowering inflation to 2% monthly. The government seems to be committed to tight monetary policy and tries to create incentives for domestic and foreign investment in the economy.

Business entities and individuals are subject to very heavy taxation in Russia. As a result there is ample evidence of an underground economy. Every business entity pays 17.5% Value-Added Tax (VAT) on its gross sales revenues. In addition, there is a business income tax, ranging from 35 to 38%.   Advertising costs are not expensed in calculating income tax and can be covered only from the company's net income.

---

[1] However, similar bars in Moscow and St. Petersburg sell draft beer at the price of 17,000-27,000 rubles per half a litre.

Personal income tax rates are significant and range up to 40%. Beer and wine are heavily taxed in comparison with liquor. Imported alcohol products are charged 10% import excise tax.

There are no recent demographic or consumption statistics for Omsk. National statistics on household income are included in the Exhibit 1. The population of Omsk is estimated at 500,000. It is considered a college town and a high proportion of residents are students or professors. Students attend school for free but extra spending money is very limited. University professors make between 135,000 and 266,000 Rubles per month; administrators 440,000 Rubles per month or more. Purchasing a condo apartment can run 110,000,000 Rubles. However, in some cases employers provide low cost housing. Even so, one's salary is usually not enough to live on. In many cases even two salaries, with both husband and wife working, may not be enough. Many residents work one or more part-time jobs. Many residents do not own cars. There are very few high-end, imported cars on the streets. However, the public transportation system is very well-developed and works quite efficiently.

Image is very important and residents tend to be unpretentious in public, although clothing styles vary greatly between younger and older generations. Inside their apartments, many have electronic equipment and quality furnishings. Russians are proud people and value their intellectual training.

Market Description

The volumes of beer, wine, and liquor consumption are not known. Russians indicate that they consume a reasonable amount of fermented beverages, although people tend to downplay alcohol consumption since it is considered shameful to abuse liquor. This makes determining possible market segments and segment size quite difficult. However, the results of a limited survey of consumers in Omsk are provided in Exhibit 2.

There is a full range of beverages available in the city, including bottled water, soft drinks, juices, wine, and liquors. The market for beer in Omsk can be segmented into imported and domestic beer. Two brands, Holsten and Beck's, explain the majority of the imported beer sold in Omsk. Several brands of Russian beer: Kolos, Omskoye, and Sibirskoye represent the most popular brands of domestic beer sold in Omsk. The quality of domestic and imported beer brands is basically the same. The major difference is in packaging. Most of the imported beer in Omsk is sold in bottles or cans which attract residents' attention due to the significant differences in package design and foreign language labels.

During the past seven years of Perestroika two new categories of people have appeared. One is people who work in the private sector through joint ventures with foreign companies, so called "New Russians" with income levels above 5,000,000 rubles per month. The opposite extreme is a new category, "low income class", making less than 500,000 rubles per month, an amount just enough to survive on. These are people working in state-owned institutions and plants. The difference in income and behavior between these two categories is highly noticeable.

"New Russians" have a taste for Italian designer clothing, German furniture, Finnish vodka, American cars, and vacations at exotic islands. These people strongly associate "good" with "expensive". The category is fond of the "Western" life style, created by "Santa Barbara" type soap operas shown on national TV for the last four years. It is considered very prestigious to drink imported beer and go to a "foreign" bar. Therefore, there is a certain tendency among "high income" residents to spend more of their free time at such bars and to buy imported beer at retail stores to impress their friends and relatives.

The "low income" residents drink mostly domestic vodka, which is sold in the range of 12,000-36,000 rubles per half a liter, and domestic beer. They prefer to drink at home, so they tend to buy bottled beer from retail stores or kiosks in the streets. In the summer people can buy domestic draft beer in special kiosks on the street (consumers bring their own containers to be filled with beer).

However, both types of Russian buyers do not consider beer as an every day beverage. People drink beer occasionally at the end of the working week or when going out with friends. Beer is more popular among the male population. Women prefer to drink wine. Even though the imported beer selection is limited it is still very popular among younger people. Older people prefer domestic beer, mostly because it is much cheaper. However, they will buy imported beer once in a while just to taste it.

It is a Russian cultural tradition to drink beer in the sauna. People love to go to saunas with friends and have a beer or two. Approximately 10% of the population goes to the sauna every week, and at least 40% every month. Recently a number of private elite saunas offering different services have emerged in Omsk.

Competitors

Domestic and imported beer is sold in a variety of Omsk retail outlets. These include restaurants, bars, retail shops, markets, saunas, and kiosks. Maria Stolychnaja stated that " the micro-brewery concept represents a major competitive advantage in drawing business away from the other restaurants and bars." Furthermore, with a 10% import excise tax on alcohol products received from other countries, there is a trend among distributors and retail stores to buy mostly domestic products. Maria's sales forecast indicates that an annual sales volume between 100,000-150,000 liters per year can be achieved each year during the next five years. She believes that the micro-brewery restaurant can be operated on a sound financial basis.

Omsk has several restaurants and bars. The foreign type bars are very rare in Omsk. Their interior and atmosphere are extremely different from those of the typical Russian bars. One of the most elite bars, the Holsten Bar, is very exclusive. The gate is locked and customers cannot gain entry unless they are known to the staff, or accompany someone who is known. Other bars are less restrictive. The Holsten Bar sells Holsten Beer on draft. There is growing interest among the public for similar establishments, although the high cost and evening cover charges prevent many residents (usually those of the "low income class") from visiting these bars.

Bottled Holsten Beer is also found in many local retail outlets, so it has a strong local presence. There is a billboard advertising Holsten Beer in one of the traffic circles at an entry to the city. The bottle indicates that the beer is imported from Germany. The price of Holsten beer varies between retail outlets but hovers near 6,500 Rubles per half liter.

Micro-brewing Process

The proposed micro-brewing process would be located on the first floor of an existing two story restaurant owned by the company in Omsk. The first floor would include both the micro-brewery and a bar that seats one-hundred people. The main dining room of the restaurant would be located on the second floor.

Two types of beer would be produced by the micro-brewery: Pilsner and Bock beer. Pilsner beer has a 5.5% alcohol content, and requires a 15 day fermentation cycle. The second beer, Bock beer, is a dark beer which would be sold during two holiday periods each year: March through May and November through December. Bock beer, having a 7 to 7.75% alcohol content, requires a longer fermentation time than

Pilsner beer.   While Pilsner beer requires 15 day fermentation cycle, Bock beer requires 27 day fermentation cycle.

The micro-brewing process involves three steps: brewing, fermenting, and storage. These steps are shown in Exhibit 3.   In the first step, brewing, three ingredients (hops, malt, and water) are processed into unfermented beer. This step is performed in a single tank and requires eight hours to complete. (See Exhibit 4 for the exact tank size under the various equipment alternatives.)

The second step, fermentation, involves converting the unfermented brew to beer using a fourth ingredient, yeast. This step is performed in a different tank and requires 15 days to complete. (See Exhibit 4 for the exact tank size and number of tanks under the various equipment alternatives.) Two eight-hour batches are brewed in a single
day (16 hours) in order to fill the fermentation tank. Under Alternative A this process consists of four fermentation tanks in total, enabling up to 4,400 liters of beer to be in process at the same time.

The third and final stage of the process is a holding stage.   There are five 1500 liter tanks which are used to store the finished beer under each investment alternative.   Beer is piped directly from these tanks to the bar area for use in serving customers.

Product Costs

There are three major components of product cost: labor, direct material, and overhead expenses.   The micro-brewery staff includes four people: two brewmasters and two laborers.   The wage rate for the brewmasters is 330,000 Rubles per month, and the wage rate for laborers is 200,000 Rubles per month. This staff would work a five-day workweek at eight hours per day, and fifty weeks per year.

It is proposed that all of the raw materials except water are to be supplied by the micro-brewery equipment manufacturer. These materials include malt, hops, and yeast. Since the equipment manufacturer is located in Germany, all supplies need to be purchased in German DM. Currently, the exchange rate is 3,260 Rubles per DM. The following prices for ingredients have been quoted by the equipment supplier: malt (.109 DM/finished liter of beer), hops (.085 DM/finished liter of beer), and yeast (.062 DM/finished liter of beer).

Overhead cost includes three items: utilities, cleaning materials, and equipment maintenance services. For the first year of operation both cleaning materials and equipment maintenance services are to be supplied by the equipment manufacturer as a part of the equipment purchase price. After the first year these items can be purchased from the equipment manufacturer. Each package of cleaning supplies costs 15.3 DM, and can be used for four (eight hour) batches in the brewing process (stage 1). After the first year the equipment manufacturer will provide maintenance services at a cost of 27,000 DM per year. The utility costs are: electricity 350 Rubles per Kilowatt, and water 1.5 Rubles per liter. 90 Kilowatts of power are used for each 1,500 litre brewing batch.

Investment Proposal

As Gregoriy Rasputin reviewed the investment proposal, he noted several items that he believed would have a major bearing on its attractiveness. First, the marketing director felt that the product and product image of the micro-brewed beer would provide an important competitive advantage in the marketplace. Therefore, she recommended pricing both the Pilsner and Bock beer at 12,000 Rubles per half Liter.   Furthermore, her sales forecast indicated that a level of between 100,000-150,000 Liters of beer could be sold each year over the next five years.

Second, the capacity of the micro-brewery process would have an important impact on its profitability. The investment and the equipment capacity in each of the five different equipment alternatives are shown in Exhibit 4. In each case the investment would cover both the processing equipment in the micro-brewery and the furniture and fixtures for the entire first floor bar.

The processing equipment includes a single brewing tank, several fermentation tanks, and five 1500 litre holding tanks. The economic life of this equipment is expected to be ten years. Under each alternative a 50% utilization rate is to be used in determining the achievable output of the micro-brewery process. This accounts for the extensive cleaning and maintenance required to sustain the correct bacteria condition in the process.

Gregoriy believed that the payback period for this investment should be no more than two years in order for the project to be competitive with other investment projects currently being considered by the company. He also knew that the Marketing Director was eager to move ahead with this project and, therefore, a decision had to be made soon.

Question for students

1)   What market segment(s) should be targeted for the micro-brewery?

2)   What marketing strategy and , specifically, what pricing policy, is appropriate for the product?

3)   What should be the capacity of the micro-brewery, i.e. what equipment alternative would you choose?

4)   Should the firm make an investment in the micro-brewery? Why or why not?

Exhibit 2

Omsk Consumer Survey Results

1. How many litres per week do you drink of:		
- Water	2.97	liters
- Soft Drinks	1.27	
- Coffee, Tea	3.44	
- Imported Beer	0.38	
- Domestic Beer	0.49	
- Imported Wine	0.17	
- Domestic Wine	0.18	
- Vodka	0.18	
- Other	0.10	
2. When do you drink beer? (1)		
- With the meal	12%	of respondents
- With friends during the day	18%	
- At restaurant or bar	6%	
- At friends	12%	
- Special occasions	18%	
- In the sauna	29%	
- Never	6%	
3. How much do you expect to pay per litre of:		
- Domestic Beer	2,300 - 5,000	Rubles
- Imported Beer	5,000-15,000	Rubles

(1) Not additive because of the particular design of the questionnaire.

Exhibit 3

Micro-brewery Process Flow Diagram

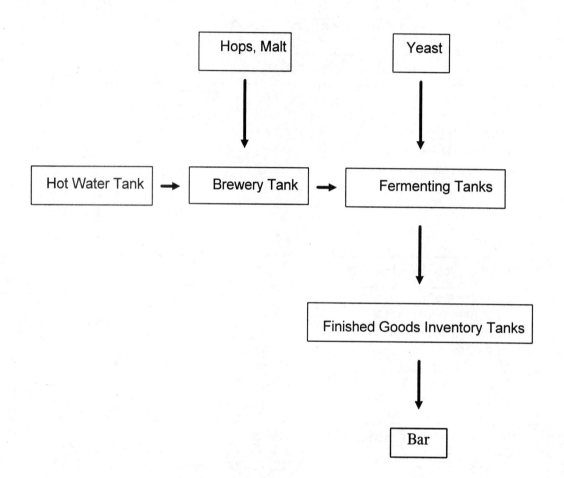

Exhibit 4

Micro-brewery Equipment Alternatives

	A	B	C	D	E
Brewing Batch Size/Tank Size (Liters)	560	1500	5000	6500	8500
Capital Investment (MM Rubles)	2,288	3,080	3,960	5,720	7,480
Number of Fermentation Tanks	4	6	8	9	11
Fermentation Batch Size/Tank Size (Liters)	1,100	3,000	10,000	13,000	17,000
Number of Brewers	1	2	2	2	2
Number of Laborers	1	2	3	4	6
Brewing Clean-up Time (Hrs)	.25	.5	.5	.75	1.00
Brewing Run Time (Hrs)	7.75	7.50	7.50	7.25	7.00

Note: The brewing process can work up to two eight hour shifts per day. The fermenting process can be run 24 hours per day.

Case 2.2

AT&T de Mexico

Summary

The necessary preoccupation of international businesses with organizational design is well illustrated through the experience of AT&T de Mexico. This case is seen through the perspective a newly assigned manager (Penny Shaffer) who was in charge of restructuring/organizational change at AT&T de Mexico early in 1995. The turbulent environment for business in global markets resulted in a dramatic change in Ms. Shafer's job assignment throughout 1995. Design issues in the spring were how to combine several independent businesses into one set of services that would have a much stronger customer focus. In September of 1995, however, AT&T decided to sell off some of the same lines of business that were part of the restructuring plan only six months prior. The case, as written, represents the market environment and strategic planning that were current as of March, 1995. From it, we see how regular restructuring of the business may be required as global markets are exploited.

In the spring of 1995, Penny Shaffer, AT&T de Mexico's Director of the newly created Process Management Department, was assigned the important task of coordinating AT&T de Mexico's organizational changes and restructuring team efforts. Shaffer was sent to Mexico from AT&T's home office after completing a number of assignments in other countries. Through reorganization AT&T hopes to allow its Mexico division to better integrate services to match growing customer needs as well as to improve overall efficiency. Shaffer's task of smooth implementation of the reorganization is complicated by various environmental circumstances.

Sales in AT&T de Mexico's five lines of business — Global Information Solutions, General Business Communication Systems, Consumer Products, Network Systems, and International Operations — are negatively affected, to different degrees, by the volatile economic market. The interest rate in 1995 is over 100% and the peso exchange rate is approximately 7 pesos to the U.S. dollar. Only months ago, interest rates were 40% and the peso was trading at 5.6 to the dollar.

Despite the current economic crisis, opportunities in the telecommunications industry are increasing. The 1994 North American Free Trade Agreement (NAFTA) has prompted the government to modernize and streamline infrastructure at a quicker pace. In order to better expand telecommunication networks, the Mexican government has agreed to open the long distance communications market in 1997.

This case was written by Amanda Spoerndle, Marlene Vaske and Panjaporn Vittayalerdpun, MBA students in 1995 in the Max M. Fisher College of Business, The Ohio State University, under the supervision of Professors Roberto Garcia, Stephen Hills, and G. Keong Leong. This case was written for class discussion and does not necessarily imply good or poor management practices.

In 1997, Telefonos de Mexico S.A. de C.V. (Telmex) will lose its monopoly on long distance service in Mexico. By introducing competition the Mexican government hopes to improve the country's communication infrastructure. The government has said it will grant licenses to offer long distance service to any company that meets the requirements. Draft regulations for licensing are overdue and were to have been issued in March 1995. Due to the current economic crisis, there is some speculation that the government may end the monopoly before 1997.

AT&T and its formidable telecommunications competitors — Ericsson (60 years in business), Alcatel (50 years), and Siemens (100 years) — from all over the industrialized world are already in Mexico selling unregulated, complementary telecommunications goods. Each is developing strategies to exploit the tremendous opportunities afforded by Mexico's growing need for telecommunications technology. Shaffer must balance the competitive advantages and disadvantages of AT&T Mexico's reorganization strategies with the company's corporate and Mexican cultures. The reorganization intends to provide more efficient customer service, product distribution, supplier control, and reduction in overlapping division functions (such as management of human resources). The opportunities for profit among the integrated AT&T Mexico divisions and regions across the U.S. border heighten the importance of creating an initial positive image of integrated telecommunications service to the Mexican consumer.

Background and History

In 1983, AT&T was a company with shares worth US$149.5 billion and more than 1 million employees. After years of fighting, the Bell Systems lost their monopoly on the telecommunications industry in the United States. On January 1, 1984, the break-up of the Bell Systems was final. The end result was the creation of seven regional telephone companies and AT&T.

Since the break-up of the Bell Systems in 1984, AT&T has undergone multiple transitions. The company has reorganized its structure as demanded by the market and has looked beyond U.S. borders for new markets. One of AT&T's goals is to generate 50% of their profits outside the U.S.. It is also integrating newly purchased corporations in order to better satisfy customer needs. For example, AT&T had (as of early 1995) acquired such companies as Actuarial Sciences Associates Inc., Tridom, Paradyne, and NCR. Another strategy has been to engage in joint ventures and it has done so with companies like Mitsubishi, NEC, and Toshiba. In addition, projects such as World-Partners provide multinational clients with communications services linked to other major long distance companies around the world.

AT&T has quickly adapted to the organizational changes that took place in 1984. In 1994, AT&T had a presence in nearly 100 countries and conducted business in over 200 countries. Employees in all divisions outside of the United States exceeded 28,100. Revenues and adjusted earnings at AT&T were up more than 15% compared to 1993. In 1993, AT&T reported global revenues of more than $68 billion. AT&T's annual investment in Bell Labs exceeded 3.4 billion dollars. Heavy involvement in researching new products and technologies could allow AT&T to take the lead role in making changes in the telecommunications industry.

AT&T in Mexico

AT&T is not completely new in the Mexican market. AT&T first entered Mexico in 1927 as a correspondent of Mexican telephone companies. In this role, it carried long distance service between Mexico and the United States. This role did not begin to expand until the late 1980's. Even as late as 1987, AT&T employed only three people in Mexico. Today, as a result of Mexico's modernization programs and AT&T's global strategies, AT&T is a source of nearly 10,000 jobs in Mexico. In addition, its sales in Mexico are greater than those of IBM and Dupont.

Although AT&T has been in Mexico many years, it is still not a widely known company. One of the company's goals is to inform the public of its lines of business and create a solid public image. In 1994, it was faced with the decision of whether to pronounce the company name "AT&T" in English or Spanish.

Despite the company's known logo recognition in Mexico, its name had never been pronounced in the electronic media. With the growth of the telecommunications industry, electronic media would be essential for promoting the company to households. Arguments in favor of a Spanish pronunciation were largely based on AT&T's experience in Puerto Rico. In Puerto Rico, it used the English pronunciation but found that when a competitor with a Spanish name entered the market, AT&T lost 60% of its market share in one week. This was largely seen as a rejection of U.S. dominance in Puerto Rico. AT&T was concerned about making the same mistake in Mexico.

There were also compelling arguments for selecting an English pronunciation. The company might be perceived as owned by Telmex if it used the Spanish pronunciation. Consumers might view the company as a poor copy of the original if it changed the pronunciation of its name. Mexicans would expect the company to have pride in its name and not to change it. Using an American name might also help AT&T to differentiate itself from other companies. Companies such as Timex had been successful in using the English pronunciation of their names and AT&T ultimately decided to follow suit.

AT&T de Mexico provides the Mexican consumer with: (1) long distance service between Mexico and the U.S., (2) fully integrated telecommunications equipment, (3) services and networking capability related to computers, (4) consumer telecommunications products, and (5) technical support and training. AT&T de Mexico also offers business translation, satellite, and capital corporation services.

In 1987, AT&T de Mexico had a simple structure with an International Operations Division and a plant in Guadalajara. Since then the company has expanded to include three other lines of business. Each new line of business has entered Mexico and operated independently of the other business units. AT&T currently operates five lines of business in Mexico:

AT&T Global Information Solutions (GIS) was formally NCR and in 1995 employed 300 people in Mexico. GIS provides computer products and systems, financial products and systems, retail products and systems, workstations, professional services, customer support services, and business forms and media. For example, it imports ATM machines and point of sale systems for sale in Mexico.

AT&T General Business Communications Systems (GBCS) has been in Mexico for two years. It sells general business equipment that provides a wide range of options for transmitting, receiving, and controlling voice, data and video messages simultaneously or through electronic registers. Country wide, GBCS in 1995 employed 150 people.

AT&T Consumer Products (CP) sells items such as telephones and answering machines to retailers and Telmex. It is currently in charge of two plants in Guadalajara, Jalisco and Monterrey, Nuevo Leon. AT&T Consumer Products exports 95% of what is manufactured in Mexico. The sales division in 1995 employed 50 people.

AT&T Network Systems (NS) produces network telecommunications equipment, including switching, transmission, cable, and wireless products. In addition, it provides software and systems integration capabilities for the world's telephone companies, governments, private network operators, and wireless services. Its largest customer is Telmex. Network systems employed 600 people in 1995.

AT&T International Operations Division (IOD) is Mexico's oldest AT&T division. It currently provides long distance service between the U.S. and Mexico. IOD terminates calls from Mexico to the U.S. while Telmex terminates calls from the U.S. to Mexico. Under this arrangement, there is a division of revenues with Telmex. In addition, it markets USA Direct to U.S. expatriates, military personnel, etc. In 1995, IOD employed 40 people.

In 1995, AT&T operated four plants, and employed a total of over 8,000 employees in these plants. In Guadalajara, Jalisco, the plant assembles telephones, answering machines, and other products. The plant in Monterrey, Nuevo Leon manufactures telephones and answering machines and, like the other plants, exports most of its products. These first two plants are under CP control. In Matamoros, Tamaulipas, AT&T Micro Electronic assembles micro electronic components and systems like transformers and power sources. These products are integrated later on in equipment such as central telephone exchanges, computers, laser printers, data transfer systems, short-wave radio transmitters, connecting cables, and cellular telephones. ATTEL del Norte is another AT&T plant, located in Reynosa, Tamaulipas. It is dedicated to backing the sales guarantee that all products are of world-class quality. Moreover, AT&T has an assembly contract with a Monterrey plant and five subcontracts with manufacturers in Sabinas, Nuevo Laredo, Nogales, Ciudad Juarez, and Reynosa.

Restructuring Plans

When AT&T began to expand globally, the corporate office encouraged each of its product divisions to go international on an individual basis. This resulted in each company entering a new market at a separate time and running a completely separate operation from the other divisions. The results are little coordination among the divisions and duplication of services. Integrating telecommunication services is expected to affect more than just the services AT&T provides. AT&T is currently working on restructuring its Mexican operations into a country unit. This will put the five lines of business under the umbrella of AT&T de Mexico (Exhibit 1).

AT&T in four other countries also uses the country unit type of organization. These four countries are: Spain, China, United Kingdom, and Germany. Penny Shaffer explains, "By fully deploying resources, customer overlap can be reduced and functions can be integrated." AT&T also hopes to create a unique public image and gain economies of scale through consolidation. Under the restructuring plan, the support services of finance, human resources, marketing, etc. will be consolidated. Currently each line of business is providing these services separately. In addition, AT&T plans on integrating customer service. This will allow an AT&T customer to call one number for service, regardless of where the product or service was purchased. This consolidation is designed to allow AT&T to provide a solid and single image of the company. In addition, restructuring is expected to push it closer towards the company vision of AT&T as "the one and the best."

The restructuring plan brings new challenges to AT&T. The uncertainty in the market, formidable existing competition, and the evolving long distance consumer market may give smaller companies a competitive advantage. The smaller companies may be more flexible to change and able to quickly exhaust niche markets. The timing of AT&T's restructuring and market volatility could present opportunity for competitors to find holes to occupy within the telecommunications industry. Smaller companies may also practice aggressive price cutting to compete.

Although the current economic situation is uncertain, it may provide an advantage to AT&T's restructuring plans in two ways. First, with business at a slower pace, the divisions have time to spend on restructuring. In a more active market, restructuring often takes second place to more pressing concerns. As it is, employees have more time to spend learning new roles in the company. Second, because the company is stretched economically, employees will be more motivated to make changes. It is often easier to motivate people to change when there are problems than when all is going well. Although the situation in Mexico is unfortunate, the opportunities provided should not be overlooked.

Restructuring will create a matrix system of management for AT&T de Mexico. Under this system, there are three reporting levels: the country level, the regional level, and the divisional level. According to Eduardo Gandarilla, President and General Director of AT&T BCS Mexico, he now spends about 50% of his time reporting to and exchanging information among his three bosses. While this form of management has been successful for some companies, such as Asea Brown and Boveri, it will provide some unique challenges for AT&T.

In addition, team building will be an important part of the restructuring process. Previously, business in Mexico was run from the top down. One challenge is that in Mexico there is a cultural bias against change. However, this is a good time to bring teams together since business is slow. Ben Cavazos, Operations and Business Development Director of AT&T de Mexico, works on team building by expanding on the company vision of "the one and the best." AT&T employees are being asked to incorporate teams into their work life. Mr. Cavazos is working on empowering his teams to better function in the new AT&T structure.

Although restructuring is expected to provide many benefits, there are also certain risks. One area of concern is that divisions may lose a degree of autonomy. Currently, the divisions are free to react quickly to market changes. Restructuring may add another layer of bureaucracy to the process. Also, will a large corporate structure be able to make sound decisions quickly? Although AT&T de Mexico will only be taking on functions that are shared across divisions, it will be required to balance the needs of all the divisions. This may lead to corporate decisions that might not fit each individual division. As stated before, a related concern is that many of AT&T's competitors are small niche companies. This leads to the question of whether or not functioning as a large "one-stop shopping" company will be effective and flexible enough in an industry dominated by niche companies.

ENVIRONMENT

Mexican Economy

On December 20, 1994, the Mexican finance minister Serra Puch announced that the exchange rate would be increased by 13%. Although he said that this did not mean that the government was devaluing the peso (N$) the markets reacted with panic. On that day $3.5 billion left the country. That night, the Central Bank of Mexico announced free floating of the new peso versus the dollar. The next day, the exchange rates opened at 5.6N$: US$1. This sparked the economic crisis that Mexico is currently experiencing. The reasons for the crisis are both political and economic. Political instability arose from the August elections, recent kidnappings and assassinations, and the Chiapas rebellion. The instability in turn caused a great deal of capital flight from the country. Seventy-five percent of the country's deficit was financed in short term debt with only 25% financed by capital investment. This made it easier for capital flight to occur as the political situation became more unstable.

The Mexican economy has been impacted in many ways since the devaluation.   Following the December crisis, the Mexican stock exchange lost 1,000 points. The value-added tax has been raised from 10 to 15%. Gas and electricity prices have risen 20%, and public sector spending will be cut by 10%. The minimum wage will rise on April 1,1995 by 10%. Interest rates currently exceed 100%. Also, an international assistance package has given Mexico US$53 billion in credit. In general, a two-to-five year period is expected before Mexico fully recovers from the crisis. Government projected for 1995 a 2% decrease in GDP, 42% inflation, and the peso trading at 6.0 to US$1. The most devastating effect of the devaluation is loss of confidence in the government.

There are two positive aspects to the devaluation. First, the currency is now being evaluated by the market and not manipulated by political strategies. Second, the export sector in Mexico is now being stimulated. In the first two months of 1995, Mexico did fairly well in foreign trade. The trade deficit was only $78 million compared to $3 billion for the same period last year. During the month of February, Mexico had a $452 billion trade surplus.

AT&T has also been affected by the crisis, although AT&T Consumer Products has been the least affected by the devaluation since it exports 95% of its products. This operating unit has, however, seen domestic sales slip as consumer demand has decreased. AT&T Global Information Solutions is expecting a 40% loss in sales.   Overall, many companies are postponing investment in telecommunications until the economy stabilizes, causing business for AT&T to slow down and contracts to be canceled. Accounts receivable, after the peso devaluation, accounted for approximately 25% of total assets. Total earnings also went down significantly.

Actions taken by AT&T to counteract the devaluation impact include: a greater than 25% price increase on all products; focus on promotion of products manufactured in the NAFTA regions to minimize margins created by the devaluation; price discounts to major retailers; and continued work with Telemex to provide long distance interconnection service and technology for new telecommunications infrastructure.

North American Free Trade Agreement

In general, NAFTA will not greatly affect the telecommunications industries in the U.S. or Canada as a result of previously formed free trade agreements between the two countries. Mexico will be required to make the majority of the changes in order to conform to NAFTA.

NAFTA has several implications for the telecommunications industry. It will not allow the participating governments to set prohibitive incorporation or licensing requirements for entering the communications industry. Mexico will be required to lower their tariffs (previously 150% higher than those in the U.S.). For example, AT&T has estimated that they would save between US$40-45 million in equipment tariffs during the first year of NAFTA. In addition, AT&T has already received US$150 million in contracts to install fiber links between Mexican cities and switching systems.

Another aspect of NAFTA is Mexico's requirement to implement standard certification of equipment. As a result, Canadian and U.S. firms will not undergo additional and time-consuming certification procedures on exports already certified in other countries. Mexico will also be obligated to lift foreign ownership restrictions on telecommunication companies.

While Mexico has been forced to make many changes due to NAFTA, the country has witnessed, and will continue to see great benefit. Since 1990, the number of phone lines in Mexico has risen 35.8%. In addition, phone service has been brought to more than 64,000 rural communities. The Mexican government has also committed to a five-year modernization plan of their telecommunications network at an estimated cost of US$ 13 billion.

Competition

The telephone market in Mexico can be divided into four lines of business: local service, long-distance service, consumer products, and other services such as information, communication, and network systems. Only AT&T is providing full lines of services and products to Mexican customers. Both AT&T and other formidable companies are recognizing the tremendous potential for profit and are moving into the market at an urgent and fierce pace. As a result of AT&T's marketing efforts in the U.S. Hispanic market, AT&T nearly tripled its spending on Hispanics from $6.7 million in 1993 to $19.2 in 1994. The advertising plans for 1995 included hiring Grammy award winner Jon Secada to do Spanish-language television commercials in February 1995 for AT&T TrueVoice. AT&T will also sponsor a nationwide radio call-in show on the CBS Americas Network called Buenas Noches America, which focuses on immigration issues. Last year, U.S. companies spent an estimated $953 million on the Hispanic market.

Telmex, the largest telephone monopoly in Mexico, occupies the local service segment. However, its service is reported to be overpriced and inefficient. Users are plagued with dead lines, wrong numbers, and false busy signals. In 1990, Telmex was privatized by the Mexican government. That same year, it went public on the New York Stock Exchange. Telmex holds a monopoly on local service well into the next century and on long-distance service until 1997. However, it has subcontracted its long-distance service to AT&T and receives a commission charge. At present, AT&T's aim is to become the second largest communications carrier in Mexico.

The Mexican government plans to end Telmex's monopoly on long distance in 1997. The showdown has begun as U.S. long distance companies line up with Mexican partners and await the draft regulations that were due out in March 1995. Competition among the three U.S.-based telecommunications competitors, AT&T, MCI, and Sprint, would heat up even further due to the tremendous potential to capitalize on the overlapping U.S. and Mexico markets. Most analysts had expected AT&T to work with Telmex. However, due to the breakup of the Bell system, there were some barriers in doing so. Because one of Telmex's owners is a Bell company, Southwestern Bell Corporation (SBC), there are legal restrictions in offering long-distance service with AT&T.

In 1994, MCI announced plans to join with Grupo Financiero Banamex Accival, while Bell Atlantic Corporation teamed up with Grupo Iusacell. GTE is aligned with Grupo Financiero Bancomer and Valores Industriales SA. Significantly, Sprint joined with the monopoly Telmex.

Although Telmex is facing the loss of its monopoly status, it is still an enormous source of competition. With $7.9 billion in revenues for 1993, Telmex is Mexico's largest company. Furthermore, it has 34% net profit margin, which is among the highest in the world. Telmex represents Mexico's largest publicly traded company with about 20% of the entire Mexican stock market capitalization. Analysts also expect earnings to grow at about 14% this year. Telmex invests more than $2 billion per year in infrastructure, an amount greater than AT&T's total investment worldwide.

AT&T & Grupo Alpha Alliance

AT&T announced a $1 billion joint venture with conglomerate Grupo Alfa. AT&T owns 49% of the new venture and Grupo Alfa owns 51%. Initially, the new company plans to target corporate customers, eventually extending services to include residential customers. Victor Pelson, AT&T's global operations chief explained, "AT&T will be offering local and long distance phone services throughout the entire country." The alliance would combine the strength of AT&T's brand, product, and service range, reputation for quality, technology, and network expertise with Alfa's broad customer base, management skills, and its record in identifying high-growth industries and entering alliances strategic to Mexico. Besides, Mr. Cavazos stated, "The most important reasons were Grupo Alfa's financial strength, its diverse business, and its excellent contact with Mexican government. The additional reason would be, they they are not in the telecommunication business."

As a $2.5 billion global company with a leadership position in a diverse portfolio of steel, petrochemical, textile, and food businesses, Alfa has 15 strategic alliances with companies in Asia, Europe, Latin America, and the United States. Its partners include Amoco, Dupont, Ford, Kawasaki, Worthington, BASF, Akzo Nobel, and Bekaert. "The advantage of our alliance is that we would offer a full range of technology solutions to a broad customer base across the entire country," said Dionisio Garza Madina, Alfa's chief executive officer. "We're working with AT&T because of its superior technology, its unparalleled commitment to quality, and its proven long-term commitment to Mexico."

AT&T's alliance with Grupo Alpha is differentiated from the other telecommunications partnerships in scope and intent as it does not limit the market to a specific customer base, technology, or city within Mexico. AT&T reports that 70 percent of calling volume in Mexico comes from residential consumers. The broadest array of technology solutions are intended to be offered in one place. None of the competitors are expected to offer the same expansive geographic, market, or technology approaches that focus on multiple markets, services, and products.

Existing Market

There is room for growth in the Mexican market. Mexico has approximately 12 telephone lines per 100 people compared to 54 per 100 in the U.S.. This number is expected to almost triple by the year 2000. The Hispanic population is rapidly increasing in the U.S.. It rose to 25.9 million in 1994 and is expected to hit 35.7 million by the year 2005, surpassing the African-American population. Residential consumer calling comprises approximately 70% of the calling volume between Mexico and the United States. Cross-border telephone traffic between the two countries accounts for more than 2 billion minutes annually and represents the second largest telecommunications traffic stream in the world. The summary of the yearly increase in the Mexican telephone market from the years of 1992 through 1998 is presented in Exhibit 2. Projected opportunities for growth in terms of yearly increase are favorable.

AT&T de Mexico's Future

While the integration of service and functional tasks offers some exciting opportunities, AT&T de Mexico also faces many challenges. Working teams are a new concept to Mexican companies and, typically, loyalty is to the individual and not to the function. This reorganization strategy may take some time to fully implement. However, since the break up of the Bell system in 1984, industry analysts have speculated that there has been no telecommunications area in which AT&T has not become a major player. Can AT&T de Mexico balance its organizational restructuring strategy and be "the one and the best" in the dynamic Mexican telecommunications industry -- even in the midst of the current Mexico economic crisis? AT&T has come fast and far with their new approach but the stakes continue to rise as developing countries open their doors and pocketbooks to new telecommunications technology. AT&T's global focus is evident in their goal of having 50% of revenues come from international operations. Mr. Gandarilla summed up this international attitude when he said that AT&T should not think of itself "as a citizen of one country, but a citizen of the world."

Questions for students

1. Contrast the market expansion strategies of AT&T with its competitors as each tries to take advantage of changes in Mexico's regulatory environment.

2. What is AT&T's strategy regarding relationships with customers in Mexico?

3. What implications does its marketing strategy have for human resources?

4. Does AT&T's market expansion strategy match well with its overall philosophy regarding customer service? Why or why not?

5. How would you evaluate AT&T's progress toward becoming not "a citizen of one country but a citizen of the world?"

Exhibit 1: Organizational Structure

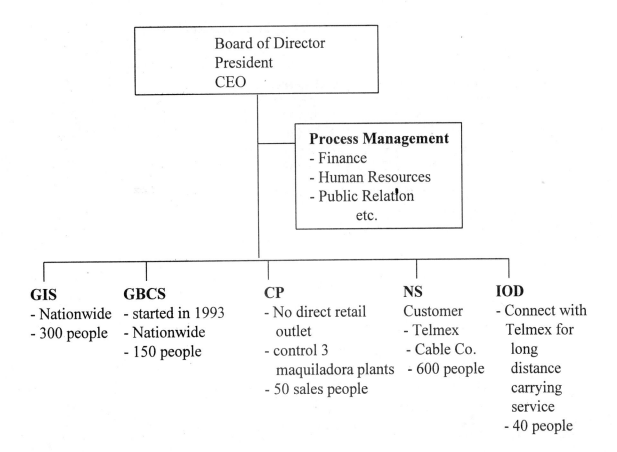

GIS = Global Information Solutions
GBCS = General Business Communication System
CP = Consumer Product
NS = Network System
IOD = International Operating Direction

Exhibit 2: Mexico Telephone Market

	Telmex	Retail	Cellular	Total Market
1992	1,610	500	109	2,219
1993	1,790	545	95	2,430
1994	1,940	580	156	2,676
1995	2,100	580	152	2,832
1996	2,250	700	243	3,193
1997	2,400	840	292	3,532
1998	2,520	1,009	348	3,877

Note : Years 1995-1998 are the forecast numbers.

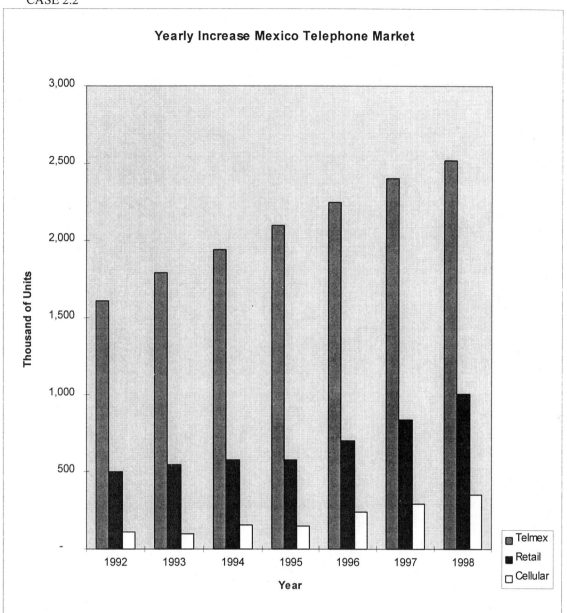

Yearly Increase Mexico Telephone Market

Case 2.3

SIBERIAN SCHOLARS' BANK

Summary

Bankers in emerging markets can face enormous challenges, especially if business rules are changing rapidly. This case examines the effects of changes in Russian policy toward the banking sector that were begun in the first year of Mikhael Gorbachev's leadership. Ten years later, a former financial Vice President of a large state owned enterprise, Tatiana Romanova, finds herself as the newly appointed president of the Tomsk Academic Town branch of the Siberian Scholars' Bank. She views her job as one of obtaining hard currency in an illiquid and constantly evolving market. Such changes include the recent implementation of a currency band around the Russian currency, the ruble, amidst an inflationary environment. The competitive environment in the formerly closed city of Tomsk is representative of that in most major Russian cities. A total of twenty nine banks do business in the city, some receiving subsidies from the Russian government and some indirectly owned by the Central Bank. Information on the competitive environment is presented and marketing strategies are discussed.

Tatiana Romanovna, President of the Siberian Scholars' Bank (SSB), faced many problems in September of 1995. As she sat in her office during an interview with an American researcher, she lamented her bank's unsuccessful efforts to attract hard currency. Without such currency, she felt her bank could not grow or compete successfully with the other twenty-eight so-called commercial banks in the Western Siberian town of Tomsk, Russia. SSB was licensed to exchange and trade hard currency, but due in part to the July 1995 Central Bank of Russia decision to create a band around the Russian ruble, the entire Russian banking industry faced a crisis of hard currency shortage. Tatiana Romanovna was surely not alone with respect to the problems and environment she encountered at work. Very few Russians were willing to sell dollars or DMs, for example, and in turn buy rubles in such a setting, where the ruble was artificially supported by Central Bank directive and foreign currency interventions. Many banks had made easy profits in the past few years with hard currency operations. The prevailing thought of most bankers was that hard currency was the key to future profitability. The president of SSB asked her new American friend for advice. "How can my bank obtain hard currency under the current circumstances?"

CHANGES IN RUSSIAN BANKING: 1985 - 1995

In order to gain a more complete understanding of Tatiana's dilemma, it would help to review the evolution of the Russian banking system from its Soviet roots to its current form. Prior to 1987, commercial banks did not exist in the Soviet Union (USSR). The Gosbank, or State Bank, was the only bank operating in the USSR. It extended "credit" to enterprises which were part of the current five-year plan. This meant that the Soviet government decided which enterprises were to receive funds and Gosbank simply carried out orders according to the plan. Most of these credits carried little to no interest and were never repaid. Such credits are commonly referred to as "soft credits."

This case was written by Tracy C. Thoman, Ph.D. candidate at The Ohio State University for class discussion and does not necessarily imply good or poor management practices.

It was in 1985 that future Nobel Prize recipient Mikhael Gorbachev instituted the first of what was to be many changes in the USSR's financial sphere. In addition to the State Bank, there were now five additional banks, all subordinate to Gosbank, created to serve distinct sectors of the economy. These were:

1. Vneshekonombank, or the Bank for Foreign Economic Affairs,
2. Promstroibank, or the Industrial and Construction Bank,
3. Agroprombank, or the Agro-Industrial Bank,
4. Zhilsotsbank, or the Bank for Housing, Community Services and Social Development, and
5. Sberbank, or the Bank for the Population's Savings and Credit.

Unfortunately, these changes were largely cosmetic in nature; the new "specialty" banks acted on orders from the State Bank, which was still mainly a conduit for budgetary flows. These banks did not act as financial intermediaries in the free market sense, transferring funds from savers to dissavers and making a profit on the interest differential, inter alia. By 1989, a few cooperative and commercial banks were allowed to appear within the Soviet Union as part of its now famous "Perestroika" (or economic restructuring) program. Most of the new banks were founded by large state-owned enterprises (SOE's) and mainly served as their financial arms. Banks extended credit to their owners in a manner similar to firms investing in certain internal projects; the difference was that no net present value analysis (or similar project valuation analysis) was typically conducted. To give the reader an idea of the monumental differences between Soviet and market economy banking, it may be helpful to realize that business clients of banks were prohibited by law from withdrawing their funds in the form of cash for anything other than wage payments. Under the Soviet system of banking, the government exercised strict control over the money supply through its banks.

It was during 1990 that Gosbank USSR separated from the 15 republic-level state banks and the five specialized banks were transformed into specialized banks operating at the level of the republics. When the USSR was abolished on December 25, 1991, all banks operating within the newly independent Russian state formed the backbone of the current Russian banking industry. Some remained specialized; others spun off into new banks with a more regional focus. Clearly, Russian banks carry a heavy historical burden during the transition in which they play an integral role.

Although estimates vary, most experts agree that there are approximately 2,500 banks operating in Russia today. This compares to the over 14,000 banks existing in the United States. Russian banks can be stratified in terms of original ownership structure as follows:

1. former specialized bank
2. spin off of a specialized bank
3. state owned enterprises
4. state social organization
5. privatized firm
6. newly private company

In other words, all Russian banks carry the legacy of their Soviet past in one form or another. Managers, employees, shareholders and customers share the culture of their communist history. This makes the transition much more complex than outside observers typically assume. Banks may be called "commercial," but that does not automatically translate into the internal restructuring necessary to ensure a consumer focus or profit orientation. In fact, only 11-12% of Russia's banks meet international standards. This is due, at least in part, to the prevalence of former communist party members and bureaucrats working as bank and enterprise presidents in contemporary Russia. The "old boy" network exists in this environment with the predictable result of loans not repaid on time, if at all. The omnipresence of nonreturned loans is a large problem for most Russian banks. The problem is magnified as the capital market is currently risky and undeveloped. Stock markets operate, but are highly inefficient. Insider trading is the rule, not the exception and shareholders, sadly, are not offered real protection or rights. Russia's financial system is moving toward a bank-centered economy rather than one based on equity. Debt is used mostly to finance development during the transition. Therefore, banks carry a heavy burden and are slated to carry Russia into a more market oriented economy.

POLITICAL - ECONOMIC RELATIONSHIP

Gorbachev's political Glasnost (openness) and economic Perestroika set the stage for Russia's current political-economic transition toward democracy and capitalism. However, as 1991's unintended dissolution of the USSR illustrated, changes in these spheres were not always coordinated or planned. As previously stated, today's Russia is a scene of former politicians running the nation's largest banks and enterprises. They often bargain with their former political colleagues for preferential laws and policies. The result of such negotiations can be seen in the following historical summary.

During 1992 and 1993, real interest rates in Russia were negative. Inflation was consistently higher than the rate the Central Bank charged on credits to commercial banks. This occurred within an environment where the ruble was free to float against foreign currencies within Russia. Banks capitalized on this situation by exchanging cheap ruble credits into hard currency (typically US dollars), then waiting and watching while the ruble depreciated relative to inflation. Foreign currency was exchanged for rubles only in amounts necessary to repay the (lower than inflation rate) loan. The Central Bank policy of negative real interest rates allowed many banks to make profits without extending loans for production or real economic activity. Billions of dollars are thought to have left the country this way, as the Central Bank continued to print more rubles.

The Central Bank Chairman was relieved of his duties in 1994 and replaced by a less politically motivated Chairwoman. Due to her policies of positive real interest rates and funding of the budget deficit by issuing government securities rather than by credit emissions, many banks no longer had the option of easy money. They are now beginning to restructure, merge with bigger banks, and declare bankruptcy, which is a new occurrence in Russia. But this process is moving cautiously. Although over 200 Russian banks were bankrupt at the beginning of 1995, the Central Bank did not revoke their licenses. It is now slowly allowing some banks to fail. Banks accustomed to crediting their owners without assessing the potential of repayment are now facing the ominous problem of nonreturned loans. August 24-25, 1995 witnessed an interbank credit market crisis: many large banks were not repaying their interbank debts. Trading stopped; banks simply didn't have the money to repay their debts on time. By October 1995, the Central Bank had revoked the licenses of 114 banks. It is certain that if the new Central Bank Chairman, appointed at the end of 1995, continues with the strict fiscal and monetary policies of his predecessor, more banks will fail in the near future. Clearly, the Central Bank as well as government level goals and policies affect the economic environment in which the banking industry operates.

CURRENCY POLICY

As noted above, the Central Bank introduced a foreign currency corridor in early July 1995. The ruble was allowed to fluctuate between 4,300 and 4,900 to the US dollar. This band was recently increased to 4,550 - 5,150. Many banks are buying dollars and DMs in expectation of the corridor floor being raised yet again. Although Russian rates of inflation have fallen recently, they remain high by international standards at 3% a month (December 1995). A protectionist economic minister was appointed in January 1996 in Russia. Inflation is widely expected to increase as this new economic czar loosens fiscal policy and increases social spending. Although the Central Bank has increased its foreign currency reserves from a mere $1 billion to $13 billion, Russia's economic chief will most likely increase barriers to trade. The result could mean retaliation by its major trading partners. Foreign reserves could be threatened by this probable decrease in exports. Many economists question how a country can keep the boundaries of exchange rate fluctuations stable in an environment of continuing inflation. Such a policy only decreases reserves, increases interest rates and poses the threat of devaluation in the near future. Mexico's December 1994 peso devaluation and currency crisis presents a powerful illustration of Russia's potential economic future.

The implementation of a currency band in Russia may help importers with cheaper foreign exchange (and therefore cheaper imports) in the short term, but it harms domestic producers, exporters and the economy in the long-term due to the artificially supported ruble. Russian products and exports become noncompetitive. Companies working in Russia must hedge their exposure to the ruble as it is certain to be devalued as inflation increases. Exports have proven to be the engine of economic growth for developing nations. The currency band could turn Russia's current trade surplus into a deficit, which could then deplete the Central Bank's foreign currency reserves. It certainly decreases the supply of foreign currency for local banks.

TOMSK COMPETITIVE ENVIRONMENT

Tomsk is one of Russia's many formerly closed cities that was opened to foreigners and other Russians in late 1991. It had been closed due to its research facilities and importance to Russia's nuclear program. The city is nearly 400 years old with approximately 500,000 residents. It is the capital city of the Tomsk region. Adjacent to the city is the academic town, Academgorodoke, which houses many of the research facilities and institutes for which Russia is known. "SSB" is short for the Siberian Scholar's Bank. Its only facility is located in Academgorodoke where its competition consists of an office of Sberbank, the State Savings bank partially owned by Russia's Central Bank.

Twenty-nine banks conduct business in Tomsk. Forty-five percent were founded in Tomsk and 55% are branches of banks located in other Russian cities, mostly the capitol, Moscow. According to economic analysts, a city the size of Tomsk, having no real industry outside of research, should not be able to support this number of banks. Tomsk has traditionally been a "budget center," meaning it lived off soft credits channeled to it by the Central Bank. Now that the Central Bank is tightening its policies, many banks in Tomsk (as throughout the entire country) are facing a difficult and uncertain environment. Four have already gone out of business; this is greater as a percentage than the failure rate in Russia as a whole. Enterprises cannot repay their debts, leaving banks with a devastating percentage of nonreturned loans.

The future of Russian banks lies largely with their management. Managers brought up in the communist tradition are not accustomed to assessing the credit worthiness of potential borrowers. Other criteria were more important, such as personal connections and amount and type of bribes offered. Some managers in the constantly changing political-economic environment of today's Russia realize that a market orientation is necessary to survive and prosper; analysis of the industry, competitors, suppliers, customers, barriers to entry and the like is only beginning to have importance for managers. But Tomsk's history as a closed city differentiates it from other more open Russian cities such as Moscow and St. Petersburg in terms of its attitude and exposure to these types of market economy principles. Managers in Tomsk are realizing at a much slower pace the necessity of a consumer focus and long-term market share than managers in cities with a more open past.

Given the legacy of most Russian banks, their managers are not schooled in the ways of a market economy. It is still common to find bank presidents in their current positions not because of their knowledge of the banking industry or transitioning economy, but due mostly to the connections they maintain with politicians and enterprise directors. Such a system makes perfect sense to most Russians. When asked what position they held prior to working as president of a bank, nearly half of Tomsk respondents answered that they were Directors of large SOEs and 25% were professors at the State University. Further, 59% were members of the Communist Party. This percentage is relatively high considering that only 17% of all Soviet citizens were party members.

Banks catering to small business in Russia have the best chances of survival during this tumultuous transition. Small firms generally do not carry the history of Soviet central planning and the mentality of soft credits like larger firms do. Many small banks have survived the most recent crisis of currency shortage in the interbank market, where banks extend loans to and borrow from each other for relatively short time periods. Large banks with less diversified loan portfolios and less flexibility were more likely to fail (during times of sudden change). While there are 82,000 large and medium-sized enterprises in Russia, small enterprises number 860,000. Smaller banks can offer better service to small businesses. SSB is a small bank by Russian standards. It would be unable to operate in most Western economies. But it can survive in Tomsk due to its niche in the academic town and the flexibility it offers its clients.

A surprising 86% of banks operating in Tomsk were founded by SOEs and/or former specialized banks. Banks of this type typically lend to their founders without considering the worth of the intended project; old habits die hard and the philosophy of "bigger is better" remains prevalent in Russian society. When asked what their strategies for the future were, an overwhelming majority of Tomsk bank presidents discussed plans for construction of larger buildings to house their offices. Appearances of "greatness" still seem to take priority over work efficiency in Tomsk. Only 36% of Tomsk banks have a marketing department, and, of these, very few use it to investigate consumer demand. Marketing activity in this environment involves advertising the bank's name or working with borrowers.

Seventy-one percent of Tomsk bank presidents would welcome government financial and technical assistance if it was considered necessary. This type of viewpoint is rooted in the uncertainty of Russia's transition. Selected banks have received Central Bank assistance with soft credits. This practice continues today and, for the most part, involves the former specialized banks and their spin-offs. The problem with such policies is that they result in continued bank dependence on the government. If the government follows Western and International Monetary Fund advice, Central Bank credit emissions will slow and eventually cease, leaving dependent banks that do not restructure insolvent, or in a position where total liabilities exceed total assets.

Two thirds of Tomsk banks do not service Russian exporters to any significant degree, even though exporters are becoming increasingly successful. The country's balance of trade ran a surplus of $20 billion in 1995. Banks who service exporters typically receive timely repayment of their loans.

In addition to the 29 legal or registered banks, there are an undetermined, but estimated large number of "informal" and illegal banks operating in Tomsk. They do not work in recognized offices; loans are granted "out of cars" and are based on an informal network of friends. Formal credit analyses are not conducted in these types of banks; loans are granted based on a client's reputation within this network. These banks lend money at much higher rates of interest due to the typically higher levels of risk associated with their loans. It can be viewed as the black market of banking and poses competition for the formal banks.

TATIANA'S DILEMMA

SSB is a branch bank founded in the Academic town of Novosibirsk, a city in Western Siberia only 120 miles away from Tomsk. Its founders are eight now privatized scientific research institutes. Shortly after the dissolution of the USSR, research institutes that weren't of high priority to Russia lost much of their funding and support from Moscow. But institutes in Tomsk have contracts to export scientific material, and are therefore able to operate efficiently without previous levels of government support. Tatiana's bank does not receive credits from the Central Bank and up to 30% of its clients are exporters. It does not currently have a marketing department and employs only 15 people. Even for Russian banks it is small. Although it does not currently have a strategic plan, it wants to form a joint venture with an American bank in the hope of obtaining hard currency.

Its president, Tatiana Romanovna, is a bright, educated and hard-working individual. She is highly qualified for her job as president of a small branch bank in Siberia. Prior to working at SSB, she was the CFO for a large SOE. Well aware of the changing environment in which her bank is operating, Tatiana is searching for ways to improve the position of her bank. She wants to attract more customers and thinks that hard currency is the key; after all, it has been the key to Russia's banking system during transition. But the level of hard currency in a bank is not necessarily associated with its reliability. Tatiana should perhaps focus upon her bank's core competence and leverage it for competitive advantage. In other words, SSB is small and can respond efficiently to the needs of its clients. Its asset base is diverse; the loan portfolio consists of credits to many firms, some of which export and therefore are more likely to return the loans. Other Tomsk banks are too large and cannot quickly service their clients. Many firms have left the larger banks for this very reason.

There are two large universities in Tomsk that offer marketing and other business courses. Due to foreign interest in this newly opened town, many non-Russian business professors and consultants have visited Tomsk and influenced its business environment. There are marketing research firms beginning operation in town. Typically, they survey residents by phone or in person; random sampling is not yet used as conditions in Siberia don't accommodate it. Tatiana needs to give some attention to the market in which she operates, but does not know how to do so. She has not asked herself where she wants the bank to be in five years: such a question does not come naturally to someone raised in a communist society. The questions she truly needs to ask do not concern foreign currency. Rather, they need to address the industry conditions in which her bank operates and how SSB can develop a niche within it. What do the consumers demand? What does SSB do better than other Tomsk banks? How can she satisfy consumer demand?

Questions for students

1.   What are the main threats facing SSB? Which are most important? Why?

2.   Is SSB prepared to confront these threats? Why or why not?

3.   Where do you think SSB should be in five years? What is its core competence and who should be its customers?

4.   Why is it a mistake for Tatiana to focus too heavily on the amount of hard currency in her bank? Why is she tempted to make this mistake?

5.   What lessons can be gleaned from Tatiana's experience that might serve as warnings for new businesses seeking credit from any of Russia's banks?

Case 2.4

STRATEGIC MARKETING CONSULTANTS (SMC)

Summary

An American retail consulting firm enters the market in Mexico, taking advantage of opportunities provided by NAFTA. Market entry for SMC is complicated by a sudden devaluation of the Peso and the subsequent decline in economic activity caused by devaluation. SMC's initial client is a Mexican retailer in competition with powerful new market entrants from the U.S. SMC must decide which innovations to suggest to the Mexican retailer that would fend off the challenge from U.S. competitors and still allow the Mexican firm to cater to Mexican customer preferences.

Strategic Marketing Consultants (SMC) is a service company in the retail consulting business. Throughout its almost 20 years of existence it has taken significant steps towards becoming a major player in strategic retail consulting. Its reputation now extends far beyond the borders of the United States.

In 1993, SMC weighed a decision to open an office in Mexico to attract new customers within the emerging Mexican market. These customers would have complemented incumbent North American customers asking for services in Mexico. Alternatively, SMC could retain its current management structure and run any Mexican consulting business through the existing two US offices.

SMC opted to enter the Mexican market as an independent consulting firm due to two main reasons. First, the firm was encouraged to enter the country because customers such as Sears requested their services in Mexico. Second, SMC was lured into the country by the opportunity to generate new, independent business. Additional support was achieved when a Mexican business person brought in two Mexican clients and offered to represent the company in Mexico. SMC subsequently set up an office in Mexico City and made Mexico a new business focus.

Before deciding, SMC had to consider several important points for and against the implementation of such a country-specific entry strategy. The following gives an overview of the company and subsequently discusses some relevant arguments with regard to its strategy. Emphasis is placed on how SMC does consulting in Mexico and on how the company successfully dealt with the difficulties of entering a foreign, previously unknown market.

Company Background

SMC has grown over time to be a highly recognized retail consulting firm. Its main office is located in the US, with one other European office. Mexico was to be its second international office. Prior to 1984, SMC had focused exclusively on traditional retail companies. It subsequently extended its services to the shopping center industry as well as to retailers of services (e.g., banks).

This case was written by Christoph Ehnert, MBA student in 1995 in the Max M. Fisher College of Business, The Ohio State University, under the supervision of Professors Roberto Garcia, Stephen Hills, and G. Keong Leong. This case was written for class discussion and does not necessarily imply good or poor management practices.

Compared to major consulting companies, SMC is small in size and more focused on a specific niche. In the strategic consulting business, SMC plays a very unique role offering both strategic retail consulting as well as strategic implementation. That is, SMC not only sells general retail consulting services but includes actual implementation through its project teams.

The project team approach makes integration of different services possible. Project teams usually include merchandisers, designers, lighting engineers, store planners, and architects. Thus, in strategic merchandising SMC does not consider itself as a group of loosely tied retail consultants. Rather, SMC employees prefer to speak of themselves as "intelligence gatherers, strategists, merchandising specialists, design consultants, and expert project managers" under one single, creative organization. Above all, SMC is able to provide customized solutions through its unique approach to strategic merchandising. SMC measures its success in terms of increased sales productivity achieved through its services; that is, it measures the value added through the implemented positioning and layout/design changes.

SMC distinguishes between different phases of its standardized consulting process, which are necessary to provide customized solutions to its clients. These are:

- *Identifying opportunities:* Through consumer research, industry research, and productivity and visual audits of the retail locations,
- *Developing strategies*: Positioning strategy, communications strategy, distribution strategy, and product and service strategy, and
- *Block Planning*: Merchandising and environmental design, and corporate identity and positioning.

SMC feels that this unique approach towards strategic merchandising is its major strength compared to competitors. This strength is further enhanced through the talent and expertise SMC personnel has accumulated over the years in offering customized retail solutions.

Mexico as a New Business Opportunity for SMC

The signing of the North American Free Trade Agreement (NAFTA) had been accomplished during the Mexican presidency of Carlos Salinas de Gortari (1988 to 1994). This agreement ensured that Mexico would open itself more to imports from the North American market by reducing tariffs and other import restrictions on US products. The retail business in Mexico was among the first to feel the influence of the North American market. The major Mexican retail chains began to import products, predominantly from the United States. Traditionally, importing had been a small niche for expensive import shops.

Incumbent Mexican retail chains such as Grupo Cifra or Comercial Mexicana experienced US-competition through new entrants such as Price Club, Kmart, and Wal-Mart. The Mexican retail market became more active and fast-paced through these new competitors. After experiencing high levels of protectionism in previous years, Mexican retail chains suddenly had reason to reorganize and line up with American joint venture partners (e.g., Grupo Cifra with Wal-Mart, or Comercial Mexicana with Price/Costco Inc.).

After NAFTA, 'strategic merchandising' suddenly became a commercial by-word of major importance for all retailers in Mexico. SMC felt it would be able to generate business in Mexico in this area, in addition to that related to American customers requesting SMC services for the Mexican market.

Factors Affecting Mexican Market Entry

Although the situation just described appeared very promising for entry into the retail consulting business in Mexico, several difficulties had to be considered and overcome.

Doing Business in Mexico

Business in Mexico requires a thorough understanding of the Mexican customer and the Mexican business environment. The business environment in Mexico differs greatly from that of the US. In Mexico, successful business depends on keeping close personal relations with business partners. Most businesses in Mexico are family-owned. Furthermore, the networks of a company and of company management have been developed over many years and are difficult to replicate. The Mexican government plays an important "paternalistic" role in supporting individual businesses and in making them successful. New companies entering Mexico face a very hard time from this perspective, as well as high start-up costs (other than for capital investments). It is usually recommended for a newcomer to find and use appropriate network contracts rather than entering without any such connections. Many market entrants rely on joint ventures to gain a thorough understanding of Mexican business. Often times, market entry also requires a reliance on Mexican managers with relevant networking experience in Mexico.

Challenges for Retail Consulting in Mexico

SMC had to be concerned about establishing credibility in Mexico, since it was offering truly niche-oriented and previously unknown consulting services. On one hand, the waking-up of Mexican retail business through NAFTA spurred interest in strategic merchandising. SMC had already gained reputation through projects for US customers. On the other hand, SMC had no significant experience in the Mexican market.

SMC needed a completely new set of expertise to deal with strategic merchandising in the Mexican retail environment. This meant finding and hiring experienced Mexican associates to do Mexico-specific customer research in order to understand the retail business in Mexico. The mistake of offering wrong products to Mexican clients through the recommendation of US-oriented solutions should be avoided. Similarly, the company's tailoring of thoroughly researched and customized solutions had to be maintained. Thus, significant service quality concerns were dominating the market entry decision. An appropriate representative and team of consultants had to be found to reduce the risk of providing low-quality services.

Uncertain Mexican Retail Environment

As a result of the protective market prior to deregulation, Mexican retail businesses were slower and less customer-oriented than similar US businesses. The recent changes in the Mexican business environment as a result of NAFTA opened up new retail opportunities through franchising, complete repositioning, and market entry, among others. However, this also meant that the future development of the Mexican retail consulting business was far less stable and predictable than SMC's traditional US business. Potential future political changes also had to be considered.

Retail Customer Characteristics in Mexico

The average Mexican retail customer needed more education to understand modern concepts of positioning, design, and layout. The Mexican population traditionally had no significant middle class. Most retailing was targeted either to the upper or lower end of the market, both of which were clearly distinguishable.

Thus, SMC had to put special emphasis on positioning its clients when researching the client's strategy and when recommending new merchandising strategies.

Future demographic developments and changes in tastes and preferences were difficult to forecast, despite the obvious trend of a growing middle class. Traditionally, middle and lower classes were the first ones to suffer in times of economic downturns. Thus, a potential negative impact on strategic merchandising was that tailored solutions might be seen as short-term and fail to attract the targeted customer group. This would ultimately affect SMC's reputation in the market place.

Mexican Retail Management

Management of Mexican companies was often very traditional and family-oriented. Although Mexican retail management was suddenly exposed to more modern retail concepts, it had to be slowly convinced of the need to find new ways to add value to its business. Management did not necessarily use economic projections to forecast business needs in the Mexican retail industry. Thus, American methods for making projections had to be adapted to Mexican concepts and resources.

Quality of Suppliers/Contractors and Intellectual Property Rights

Two other potential problems SMC faced in offering its consulting services to Mexican customers were the quality of local suppliers/contractors and the problem of intellectual property rights with regard to design and layout issues.

In order to provide customized solutions, SMC would need to provide integrated services in Mexico. It was deemed necessary to apply the same three-step process concept (as described above for the US market). Thus, implementation of the strategic recommendations required the Mexican project teams to find adequate contractors and suppliers, or to develop the skills to work with the contractors and personnel provided by the client.

The weak enforcement of intellectual property rights in Mexico potentially made the Mexican market less attractive to SMC by allowing SMC's competitors to replicate its work at low cost.

SMC Decides to Enter the Market

In 1993, SMC finally decided to establish itself in Mexico City through a formal representative. It rented office space with very short lease contract terms. A Mexican industrial manager offered the essential links for SMC in terms of "contacts" and "culture". Project support was provided through US-based project managers, who were native speakers of the Spanish language and familiar with Latin American business practices.

SMC enjoyed success in generating new business in Mexico with its American customers (e.g., Sears department stores) as well as with Mexican customers (e.g., Deportes Marti, a sporting goods retailer, or Banco del Sureste, a national bank). SMC's "Hispanic" connection, with its Mexican representative and its Latin-American project managers, became essential for doing business in Mexico.

The success of SMC's market entry strategy and the acceptance of its consulting services can be highlighted through its experience with one of its Mexican clients. Comercial Mexicana is a Mexican firm operating large discount/grocery stores. The many problems SMC had to face when entering the Mexican market are reflected in this case.

Comercial Mexicana — A Mexican Client

Soon after the retail business in Mexico became more accessible for outside products and competitors, Comercial Mexicana realized it needed support to remain competitive in the Mexican retail business. Incumbent retailers in the discount and food retail industry were teaming up with American joint venture partners. Also, new American entrants with innovative concepts focused on the Mexican consumer were becoming visible. Comercial Mexicana decided to hire SMC.

Organizational Issues

SMC immediately faced difficulties in finding appropriate contacts within Commercial Mexicana for information and to proceed with strategic discussions and implementation issues. All decision making and outside contacts were focused on top management. Comercial Mexicana, being a family-run business with a very hierarchical organization, was not immediately ready to accept outsiders to define and change business goals.

Furthermore, Comercial Mexicana initially resisted the idea of SMC providing services to Wal-Mart in the US, as Wal-Mart was a joint venture partner with their main competitor Grupo Cifra. Comercial Mexicana finally accepted that the consulting industry typically keeps the exclusivity rights and does not share them with the client. Solving these issues and communicating with client management was significantly enhanced for SMC by having people on hand familiar with Mexican business practices.

The New Project

SMC, however, had to adjust its style of consulting to work more toward client requirements than it was used to. SMC was not entirely independent in its recommendations and in implementation issues. For example, Comercial Mexicana confronted SMC with a predetermined site for a new hypermarket prototype in Guadalajara, Jalisco. Also, SMC had to use Comercial Mexicana construction crews and subcontractors.

The SMC team reviewed market positioning, competitive information, and economic forecasts with Comercial Mexicana executives. SMC identified "a need to increase product offering, improve store layout and design, develop in-store merchandising, and create a target image of value, volume, variety, and low prices."[1] The new hypermarket stores were meant to defend Comercial Mexicana against increasing competition from the US (particularly arising from the Grupo Cifra joint venture with Wal-Mart) and to build up an image of a strong and well-positioned retailer.

Subsequently, the SMC team dealt with the implementation issues of the merchandising strategy. It worked together with Comercial Mexicana contractors, construction crews, store management and employees.

---

[1] Retail Update (SMC Publication): "Mexican Retailer Prepares For Potential US Invasion", Winter / Spring 1994, p. 1

Layout of the New Hypermarket

Designing a new layout for the hypermarket's interior that would appeal to Mexican customers' needs was a very challenging task for SMC. The Mexican customer differs from the American one with regard to their grocery shopping needs. The grocery department had to be the central focus of the layout concept, since Mexican customers were used to doing grocery shopping on a daily basis.

SMC opted to design a hypermarket with wide alleys (racetracks) and a clear emphasis on the produce department, located toward the rear of the store. This layout was meant to draw customer attention to various product lines along their way to the produce department. Huge canopies were added to emphasize the various product lines along the racetrack. Large sections along the main alleys suggested sales promotions. These sections were used to increase the purchase frequency of items that customers did not initially intend to buy upon entering the store (impulse items).

Overall, the concept itself responded to different customer needs in Mexico. Basically, the concept resembled old-fashioned, simple store layout designs of the US (1970s). The hypermarket kept the Comercial Mexicana pelican logo, although the name of the store was changed to 'Mega Mercado' (later changed to 'Mega'). These features emphasized tradition and ensured that the Mega Mercado found wide acceptance among Mexican consumers.

Store Employees and Management

SMC provided merchandising seminars and on-site audits for employees. These were carried out to ensure an ongoing understanding of the store layout and of its integrated attention-drawing concepts. However, SMC faced a real challenge in effectively training the hypermarket's sales force. Although the workforce had a high educational level, the strong hierarchy among store personnel created communication problems.

The hierarchical differences among different employees working within the store could not be entirely overcome. Store management expected that policies would begin with and be disseminated through them. But information was not transferred to the employees responsible, and a high level of asymmetric information remained.

Careful and continuous on-site explanation of the sales-promotion layout was necessary to convince personnel to deviate from prior working habits. Reluctance to change was common among Mexican employees because of job insecurity. Overall, it was difficult to teach employees to maintain the integrity of the design on an ongoing basis. Labor union demands for detailed job descriptions increased the difficulties.

Copyright Problems of the Mega Mercado Concept

Soon after the new store opened, SMC found that its concept had been copied by a different company in one of their stores. Comercial Mexicana management erroneously assumed that SMC had provided services to its competitor and, therefore, complained to SMC. SMC considered suing the Comercial Mexicana competitor for copyright infringement. However, no legal steps were taken against the competitor because Comercial Mexicana advised SMC not to do so. Such a case of copyright infringement was considered a fairly common and unprovable business practice in Mexico.

The Peso Devaluation — Final Outlook

The Mexican currency devaluation in December 1994 hit the retail industry hard. Wal-Mart was the first to announce the (temporary) halt of its investment plans by canceling the opening of several new stores. Most other competitors, smaller in size, also reduced the scale of their investments.

SMC, as a result of its Mexican business, was directly affected by currency exchange losses of about $50,000. Because it was working on projects with large up-front payments, SMC did not suffer other immediate financial effects.

However, a longer term impact was felt due to the greatly reduced business with clients in Mexico throughout 1995. SMC faced a risk of contractual discontinuity. SMC's strategy after the peso devaluation included a rather aggressive program for new prospects. SMC suggested to its clients that the post-devaluation period was the best time to invest, allowing retailers to differentiate themselves from slower-moving competitors.

Questions for students

1. Entering new markets requires careful preliminary research but also continuous learning about world-wide markets. What evidence of continuous learning can you see in ABC's experience in Mexico?

2. How well do you think ABC did in balancing the cultural preferences of its workforce and customers with the firm's necessity to adapt to competitive pressures?

3. What specific cultural attributes made consulting with Comercial Mexicana different than might have been the case with an American client?

Case 2.5

The Information Technology Industry in India

Summary

The information industry in India was, until recently in a nascent stage. Now the industry appears to be positioned for rapid growth. This case documents the growth of the industry until now, the government's support of the industry, and the choices to be made in the future. Students are asked to consider which among several possible markets would be most attractive for firms that wish to produce software in India, both for export and for sale domestically.

In India a viable domestic market for software is just now being established. In 1992 India's domestic software market expanded 45% to US$112 million, while software exports grew by 67% to US$144 million. The export boom will be helped by new government incentives such as tax breaks and special duty free export processing zones for software marketers. India has also liberalized joint venture ownership rules, which, together with the emerging domestic market have spurred multi-national corporations (MNCs) to expand operations in their Indian subsidiaries.

Computer Hardware

The information technology industry in India has recorded an annual average growth rate of 25% since July 1991. Some of the biggest firms have set up manufacturing facilities and trading offices in India. The hardware market in India was established at US$1 billion in 1994 (see Exhibits 1 and 2). Personal computer (PC) sales of US$180,000 represented only 1% of total worldwide sales. However, this figure is expected to reach US$1 million by the end of this century. Approximately 600,000 PCs are in use in India, and nearly 20% of these are connected to Local Area Networks (LANs). Most networking is in the UNIX and Netware segments. The UNIX segment serves primarily the computer-aided design/computer-aided manufacturing (CAD/CAM) and database users. While PCs still dominate the hardware market, LAN server sales are growing rapidly. The growth rate in 1993-94 in the LAN server segment was 152%. The major customers for LANs are public sector organizations like the nationalized bank.

Indian computer companies have formed strategic alliances with major foreign players to meet the changing demand of Indian consumers. The country's largest computer manufacturer has allied itself with a major U.S. based company. The second largest company has joined forces with a top-ranking Taiwanese firm. India's hardware expertise is in design and integration of computers rather than components manufacturing. Peripherals such as keyboards, floppy drives, power supplies and printers are being manufactured in India.

Computer chip manufacturing activity is quite low in India. Approximately 50% of the chips in India are smuggled illegally from Singapore, Hong Kong and Taiwan. The duty on imported chips was reduced from 111% in 1993 to 61% in 1994. Despite this reduction, the black market continues to flourish. The pentium

This case was prepared by Professors Karthikeyan Ganesan of Anna University, Madras, India, Stephen Hills, and G. Keong Leong of The Ohio State University for class discussion and does not necessarily imply either good or poor management practices.

chip costs nearly US$1770 in India. Unless the import duty is lowered to 10% or less, illegal smuggling and the black market will continue to exist.

Human Resources & Information Technology

India has a comparative advantage in software development because of the availability of highly trained programmers. The socialist policies of the Indian government have resulted in unusually high investment in education, particularly higher education. Tuition fees in the majority of India's premier engineering, medical and management institutions do not exceed US$500 annually. As a result, quality education is available to a wide range of people, irrespective of their financial background. Education through high school is compulsory and is subsidized by the central and state governments. India has a literacy rate of 52% (male-63%; female-39%) and has the third largest English speaking population in the world (behind the U.S. and U.K.).

Programmers receive certification from numerous software training institutions throughout the country, which require only a high school diploma for students to be enrolled. More than 200,000 students are enrolled in these programs.

India has tried, unsuccessfully, to control "brain drain" of technical personnel to the United States and the Persian Gulf region. It is estimated that 80% of the technically trained graduates from the premier engineering and science and technology institutions leave the country every year. Economic liberalization is expected to lessen this trend, since executive remuneration in Indian companies is growing at a fast rate.

The city of Bangalore in the southern part of the country is popularly known as the "Silicon Valley" of India. Once the southern outpost of the British army, Bangalore has been home for a number of India's defense industries. The National Aeronautic Laboratory, the Indian Space Research Institute and the Electronic and Radar Development Establishment are all located in Bangalore. The _Economist_ reported in May 1991, that 43 engineering colleges, 52 polytechnics, and 24 industrial-training institutes were in the state of Karnataka of which Bangalore is the capital.

In 1986, a west coast U.S. firm opened an export-oriented subsidiary there. All the software, designs and databases produced by the subsidiary were exported to the parent company via satellite link. When programmers in the U.S. left for the day, their counterparts in India would log on using the satellite link. The success of the operation brought many other similar arrangements to Bangalore.

The government has recognized the potential of software export as a valuable foreign exchange earner and has created incentives to encourage this. Software Technology Parks (STPs) have been set up in various cities (see Exhibit 3). The STPs contain a centralized computing facility along with multiple dedicated satellite links to companies operating within the boundaries of the STP. Software export profits are not taxed, making the industry more attractive to investors.

At the center of growth and industrialization in India is the city of Hyderabad. The city of learning, as Hyderabad is known in academic circles, has eight universities and 28 national research centers. The state government is setting up an INFOCITY to provide all necessary infrastructure for the software industry. Software exports from Hyderabad have grown at a rate of 100% in the last four years and are expected to exceed US$1 million in 1995-1996. The city is well connected by all major national and international routes.

Information Technology Export Areas

India's software export companies have typically taken one of three forms:

- *Outsourcing*: contract all or a major part of information technology needs to Indian companies,
- *Joint Ventures*: establish relationships which service the domestic market as well as produce software solutions for export to the West, and
- *Direct Exports*: software houses export solutions directly using western companies as intermediaries.

A huge advantage for India is its ability to offer a wide spectrum of software services, from clerical support and data processing to sophisticated software systems. The services of two software companies offer examples which illustrate the rapid growth of the software industry in India.

In developed countries, technical support is extremely labor intensive and requires highly skilled computer personnel. Also, many software companies would prefer not to invest more on technical support because of its low profitability. However, a Bangalore-based software company, whose 45 employees call themselves "mentors to the globe," has carved a niche in the technical support market. This company's employees scan the various technical forums, such as those on the internet, and offer support for the problems listed. The company initially did this free of charge via a satellite link. Their reputation enabled the company to negotiate contracts with software companies, providing them with technical support at comparatively low rates.

At the other end of the spectrum is Pentafour Software, India's third largest software exporter. The company has been developing software on IBM and HP platforms and is known for its imaging technology.

In India today, 450 companies employing 7,500 people are engaged in the business of software development, the vast majority of which is focused on exports. One of the earlier entries in the software development market was the joint venture Tata-Burroughs formed in 1976 between the Burroughs and Bombay Corporation. Today, Tata-burroughs has become Tata Unisys Ltd. and employs 1150 people.

Information Technology- Current Focus

India has traditionally resisted automation due to pro-labor policies adopted by successive governments. The Information Technology (IT) industry received its initial boost in 1986 when the government reduced duties on imported computer components. The computer manufacturing industry grew rapidly, with many companies diversifying into computer assembly. Following the dismantling of the licensing system in 1991, foreign manufacturing companies began to invest in India.

Software exports have helped to sustain the growth of the IT industry in India. Since 1988, this industry has grown at an annual rate of 30%. There are no visible signs of abatement in that growth rate. Foreign companies have chosen India for software development due to its high quality, low cost work force. The salaries of American programmers, for example, are six to seven times higher than Indian salaries. The largest pool of software expertise outside the U.S. is in India. (Computergram International,11/30/94)

The customer base for hardware is split equally between government and the private sector. The adoption of information technology is slow in many government agencies, especially at the regional level. Though agencies invest in computers, they use them mainly for word processing. Due to hiring freezes, many government agencies are unable to hire computer professionals.

Computers have a longer useful life in India than in other developed countries. Due to the low cost of maintenance and high cost of new hardware, Indian professionals tend to use the same computers for many years. The high cost of hardware forces programmers to develop cost-effective and efficient programs to maximize their equipment. Crucial for India will be its ability to leap over many intermediate technologies, using only the latest.

Information Technology-Future Growth Areas

State and City Administration

The advantages of computerization remain a pipe dream for a large majority of village administrations. But with current developments in transport, power and telecommunication, computerization for villages may become viable in the not too distant future.

Tourism/Entertainment Sector

The tourism/entertainment sector presents further opportunity in the area of new product development. In cinema, the single largest revenue earner in the country, the software applications for choosing actors, actresses or models for commercials, etc., are enormous. In the area of tourism, the development of software products for guiding tourists to vacation destinations is a possibility. A large market also exists for software for musical applications for the composition and recording of Carnatic and Hindustani classical music and songs in local dialects. An increase in TV viewing and the availability of many local broadcasting channels opens further possibilities. The potential of multi-media offers still other possibilities, ranging from education to entertainment.

Summary

Since the present Indian Prime Minister's government embraced an expanded free market philosophy in 1991, U.S. firms have been leading investors in many of the nation's critical sectors, from new power plants and telephone systems to ventures that will provide fresh choices in breakfast cereals, computers and soft drinks. Many U.S. executives acknowledge that what attracted them to India was the size of the nation's population, roughly 890 million people. The Indian government estimates that approximately 200 million people belong to the middle class, with surplus incomes that make them potential customers for many foreign products. Other positive factors include the fact that India is a democracy, with independent courts to settle legal disputes, and that English is used widely in business.

U.S. exports to India have risen in the last few years. In 1990 U.S. exports to India totaled US$2.5 billion, while U.S. imports totaled US$32 billion. The best export prospects for U.S. firms are in sectors that complement India's economic development priorities, including aviation and avionics, oil and gas equipment and services, specialized industrial machinery, scientific and control instrumentation, power generation and transmission equipment, computers, telecommunications, fertilizers and metal scrap.

Impact on Global Competition

Following the liberalization which began in 1991, India became one of the world's largest emerging markets. At the same time the government, realizing the importance of information technology, reduced import duties and excise taxes on fax machines and computers. These items were previously considered luxuries and taxed at the highest possible rates.

Computers have now become affordable, not only to businesses but to the average middle class consumer. As computer sales grow, so does an industry built around technical support for software and hardware. The availability of vast numbers of technical personnel makes India a buyer's market in regard to competitive costs.

Questions for students

1.   From your first impressions, which do you think are the most profitable market segments in India's information technology industry?

2.   Would you want to undertake fairly extensive market research before entering the information technology market in India? Why or why not?

3.   Prepare an action plan for developing a niche market for personal computers. Are the distribution channels sufficient for the niche you suggest? Why or why not?

4.   If you were to search for a local firm to be a partner in developing a niche market for personal computers, what characteristics would you want your partner to have?

148

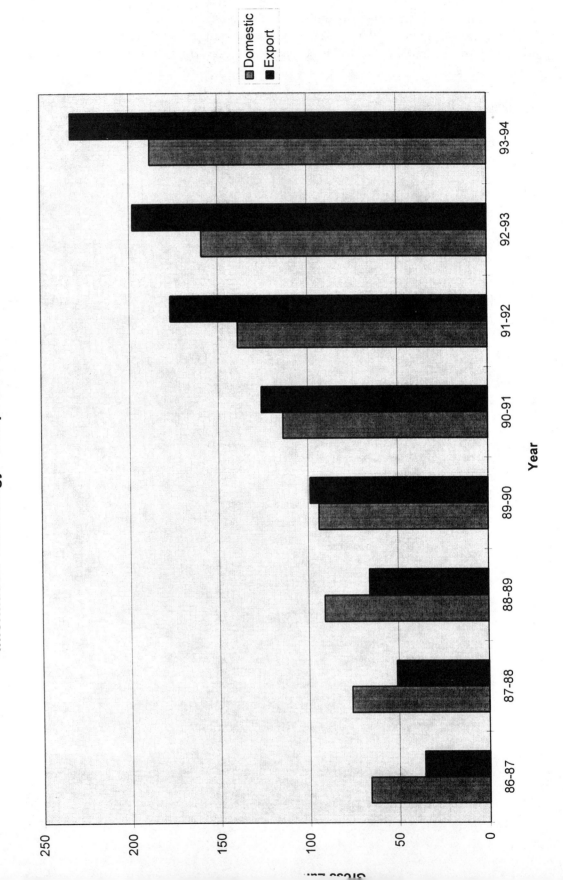

EXHIBIT 1

Information Technology - Computer Software Trends

EXHIBIT 2

Information Technology - Computer Hardware Trends

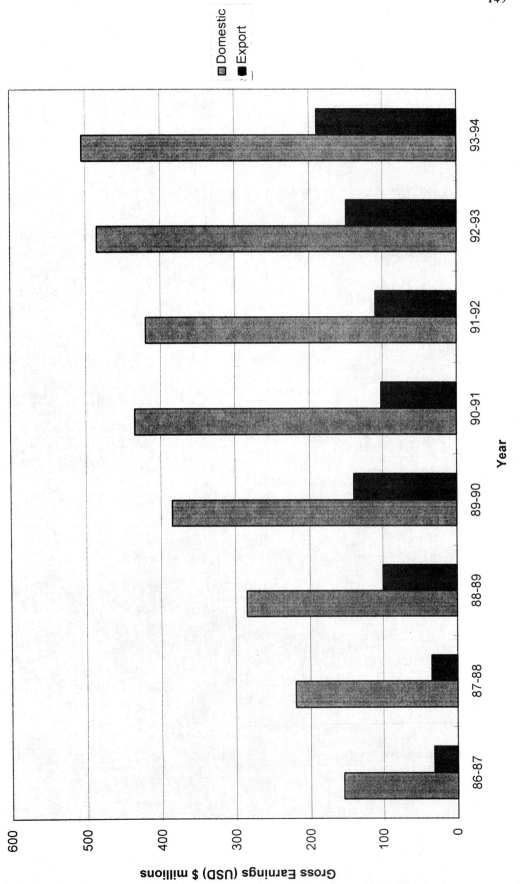

Exhibit 3

SOFTWARE COMPANIES, EXPORT ZONES AND TECHNOLOGY PARKS

Cities Where Software Companies are Based

Chandigarh	Calcutta
Delhi	Bombay
Jaipur	Pune
Lucknow	Hyderabad
Patna	Agra
Gandhinagar	Bangalore
Ahmedabad	Coimbatore
Bhopal	Madras
Cochin	Travindrum

Export Processing Zones

Delhi
Kandla
Calcutta
Bombay
Cochin
Madras

Software Technology Parks

Delhi
Gandhinagar
Pune
Hyderabad
Bhubaneshwar
Bangalore
Trivandrum

Proposed Software Technology Parks

Chandigarh
Gurgaon
Jaipur
Lucknow
Guwahati
Patna
Bhopal
Calcutta

American Computer Companies in India

Texas Instruments	Design and software of integrated circuits
Motorola	Software Development
Hughes Software Systems	Telecom software
Hewlett-Packard	R&D for Hewlett-Packard, special products for clients
IBM	Core software for IBM, banking software
Oracle Software India	Distribution, consultancy, application tools, training
Onward Novell	Product development, distribution of Novell products and training